C-987   **CAREER EXAMINATION SERIES**

*This is your
PASSBOOK for...*

Psychiatric Social Worker

*Test Preparation Study Guide
Questions & Answers*

COPYRIGHT NOTICE

This book is SOLELY intended for, is sold ONLY to, and its use is RESTRICTED to individual, bona fide applicants or candidates who qualify by virtue of having seriously filed applications for appropriate license, certificate, professional and/or promotional advancement, higher school matriculation, scholarship, or other legitimate requirements of education and/or governmental authorities.

This book is NOT intended for use, class instruction, tutoring, training, duplication, copying, reprinting, excerption, or adaptation, etc., by:

1) Other publishers
2) Proprietors and/or Instructors of "Coaching" and/or Preparatory Courses
3) Personnel and/or Training Divisions of commercial, industrial, and governmental organizations
4) Schools, colleges, or universities and/or their departments and staffs, including teachers and other personnel
5) Testing Agencies or Bureaus
6) Study groups which seek by the purchase of a single volume to copy and/or duplicate and/or adapt this material for use by the group as a whole without having purchased individual volumes for each of the members of the group
7) Et al.

Such persons would be in violation of appropriate Federal and State statutes.

PROVISION OF LICENSING AGREEMENTS – Recognized educational, commercial, industrial, and governmental institutions and organizations, and others legitimately engaged in educational pursuits, including training, testing, and measurement activities, may address request for a licensing agreement to the copyright owners, who will determine whether, and under what conditions, including fees and charges, the materials in this book may be used them. In other words, a licensing facility exists for the legitimate use of the material in this book on other than an individual basis. However, it is asseverated and affirmed here that the material in this book CANNOT be used without the receipt of the express permission of such a licensing agreement from the Publishers. Inquiries re licensing should be addressed to the company, attention rights and permissions department.

All rights reserved, including the right of reproduction in whole or in part, in any form or by any means, electronic or mechanical, including photocopying, recording, or by any information storage and retrieval system, without permission in writing from the Publisher.

Copyright © 2024 by
National Learning Corporation

212 Michael Drive, Syosset, NY 11791
(516) 921-8888 • www.passbooks.com
E-mail: info@passbooks.com

PUBLISHED IN THE UNITED STATES OF AMERICA

PASSBOOK® SERIES

THE *PASSBOOK® SERIES* has been created to prepare applicants and candidates for the ultimate academic battlefield – the examination room.

At some time in our lives, each and every one of us may be required to take an examination – for validation, matriculation, admission, qualification, registration, certification, or licensure.

Based on the assumption that every applicant or candidate has met the basic formal educational standards, has taken the required number of courses, and read the necessary texts, the *PASSBOOK® SERIES* furnishes the one special preparation which may assure passing with confidence, instead of failing with insecurity. Examination questions – together with answers – are furnished as the basic vehicle for study so that the mysteries of the examination and its compounding difficulties may be eliminated or diminished by a sure method.

This book is meant to help you pass your examination provided that you qualify and are serious in your objective.

The entire field is reviewed through the huge store of content information which is succinctly presented through a provocative and challenging approach – the question-and-answer method.

A climate of success is established by furnishing the correct answers at the end of each test.

You soon learn to recognize types of questions, forms of questions, and patterns of questioning. You may even begin to anticipate expected outcomes.

You perceive that many questions are repeated or adapted so that you can gain acute insights, which may enable you to score many sure points.

You learn how to confront new questions, or types of questions, and to attack them confidently and work out the correct answers.

You note objectives and emphases, and recognize pitfalls and dangers, so that you may make positive educational adjustments.

Moreover, you are kept fully informed in relation to new concepts, methods, practices, and directions in the field.

You discover that you are actually taking the examination all the time: you are preparing for the examination by "taking" an examination, not by reading extraneous and/or supererogatory textbooks.

In short, this PASSBOOK®, used directedly, should be an important factor in helping you to pass your test.

PSYCHIATRIC SOCIAL WORKER

DUTIES:
Collaborates as a member of a diagnostic and therapeutic team and carries out, under the direction of a psychiatrist, casework services to the emotionally, mentally, or otherwise disturbed or handicapped patient.

As a Psychiatric Social Worker, you would be assigned to a residential or a community setting in the role of a client advocate. Your duties would include admissions assessing, interviewing, referrals, placements, as well as individual, family, and group counseling. You might be required to interact with various social services and community agencies and with citizens groups. You may also be required to supervise lower-level staff; performs related duties as required.

TYPICAL WORK ACTIVITIES:
Participates in the intake and screening of new patients, evaluating and diagnosing the patient and problems; Participates as a team member in individual, group and family therapy; Provide social work services to help patients adjust to their disabilities and social environment and symptom management; Refers clients to other governmental and non-governmental agencies; Coordinates various activity and treatment programs with other agencies; Maintains and complies case records, recording pertinent information; Plans with the community mental health team and with community agencies to relate the patient's treatment and rehabilitation program to his social situation prior to his discharge; Collects and maintains appropriate data from various sources such as professional staff and patients' families to establish an overall approach to the treatment of patients' mental and social problems; Maintains information on community and health resources which can be utilized during the patient's care and subsequent to his discharge; Participates In the process of transfer of patients to other levels of treatment as appropriate; May provide individual and/or group supervision to Alcoholism/Substance Abuse Counselors; Interviews clients in their homes, correctional facilities, or clinical settings and consults with other agencies to determines client needs; Collects and maintains appropriate data from various sources such as professional staff and patients' families; Determines overall approach to solution of patients' clinical and social problems; Updates client functional assessments and service plans on a regular basis; Maintains information on community and health resources for client referrals; Participates as a team member in conferences designed for the diagnosis and treatment of clients; Monitors client progress to ensure their needs are being addressed; Writes progress reports for the client's medical record; Provides emotional and psychological support and guidance to clients; Advocates for clients in legal, financial, and/or housing matters; Coordinates multi-agency involvement with clients; May transport clients with no other means of transportation for medical and legal appointments, food shopping, recreational programs, etc .

SCOPE OF THE EXAMINATION
The multiple-choice written test will cover knowledge, skills, and/or abilities in such areas as:
1. Characteristics and problems of individuals with mental illness;
2. Developing & implementing treatment in a social work program;
3. Individual and group counseling; and
4. Preparing written material;

HOW TO TAKE A TEST

I. YOU MUST PASS AN EXAMINATION

A. *WHAT EVERY CANDIDATE SHOULD KNOW*

Examination applicants often ask us for help in preparing for the written test. What can I study in advance? What kinds of questions will be asked? How will the test be given? How will the papers be graded?

As an applicant for a civil service examination, you may be wondering about some of these things. Our purpose here is to suggest effective methods of advance study and to describe civil service examinations.

Your chances for success on this examination can be increased if you know how to prepare. Those "pre-examination jitters" can be reduced if you know what to expect. You can even experience an adventure in good citizenship if you know why civil service exams are given.

B. *WHY ARE CIVIL SERVICE EXAMINATIONS GIVEN?*

Civil service examinations are important to you in two ways. As a citizen, you want public jobs filled by employees who know how to do their work. As a job seeker, you want a fair chance to compete for that job on an equal footing with other candidates. The best-known means of accomplishing this two-fold goal is the competitive examination.

Exams are widely publicized throughout the nation. They may be administered for jobs in federal, state, city, municipal, town or village governments or agencies.

Any citizen may apply, with some limitations, such as the age or residence of applicants. Your experience and education may be reviewed to see whether you meet the requirements for the particular examination. When these requirements exist, they are reasonable and applied consistently to all applicants. Thus, a competitive examination may cause you some uneasiness now, but it is your privilege and safeguard.

C. *HOW ARE CIVIL SERVICE EXAMS DEVELOPED?*

Examinations are carefully written by trained technicians who are specialists in the field known as "psychological measurement," in consultation with recognized authorities in the field of work that the test will cover. These experts recommend the subject matter areas or skills to be tested; only those knowledges or skills important to your success on the job are included. The most reliable books and source materials available are used as references. Together, the experts and technicians judge the difficulty level of the questions.

Test technicians know how to phrase questions so that the problem is clearly stated. Their ethics do not permit "trick" or "catch" questions. Questions may have been tried out on sample groups, or subjected to statistical analysis, to determine their usefulness.

Written tests are often used in combination with performance tests, ratings of training and experience, and oral interviews. All of these measures combine to form the best-known means of finding the right person for the right job.

II. HOW TO PASS THE WRITTEN TEST

A. NATURE OF THE EXAMINATION

To prepare intelligently for civil service examinations, you should know how they differ from school examinations you have taken. In school you were assigned certain definite pages to read or subjects to cover. The examination questions were quite detailed and usually emphasized memory. Civil service exams, on the other hand, try to discover your present ability to perform the duties of a position, plus your potentiality to learn these duties. In other words, a civil service exam attempts to predict how successful you will be. Questions cover such a broad area that they cannot be as minute and detailed as school exam questions.

In the public service similar kinds of work, or positions, are grouped together in one "class." This process is known as *position-classification*. All the positions in a class are paid according to the salary range for that class. One class title covers all of these positions, and they are all tested by the same examination.

B. FOUR BASIC STEPS

1) Study the announcement

How, then, can you know what subjects to study? Our best answer is: "Learn as much as possible about the class of positions for which you've applied." The exam will test the knowledge, skills and abilities needed to do the work.

Your most valuable source of information about the position you want is the official exam announcement. This announcement lists the training and experience qualifications. Check these standards and apply only if you come reasonably close to meeting them.

The brief description of the position in the examination announcement offers some clues to the subjects which will be tested. Think about the job itself. Review the duties in your mind. Can you perform them, or are there some in which you are rusty? Fill in the blank spots in your preparation.

Many jurisdictions preview the written test in the exam announcement by including a section called "Knowledge and Abilities Required," "Scope of the Examination," or some similar heading. Here you will find out specifically what fields will be tested.

2) Review your own background

Once you learn in general what the position is all about, and what you need to know to do the work, ask yourself which subjects you already know fairly well and which need improvement. You may wonder whether to concentrate on improving your strong areas or on building some background in your fields of weakness. When the announcement has specified "some knowledge" or "considerable knowledge," or has used adjectives like "beginning principles of..." or "advanced ... methods," you can get a clue as to the number and difficulty of questions to be asked in any given field. More questions, and hence broader coverage, would be included for those subjects which are more important in the work. Now weigh your strengths and weaknesses against the job requirements and prepare accordingly.

3) Determine the level of the position

Another way to tell how intensively you should prepare is to understand the level of the job for which you are applying. Is it the entering level? In other words, is this the position in which beginners in a field of work are hired? Or is it an intermediate or advanced level? Sometimes this is indicated by such words as "Junior" or "Senior" in the class title. Other jurisdictions use Roman numerals to designate the level – Clerk I, Clerk II, for example. The word "Supervisor" sometimes appears in the title. If the level is not indicated by the title, check the description of duties. Will you be working under very close supervision, or will you have responsibility for independent decisions in this work?

4) Choose appropriate study materials

Now that you know the subjects to be examined and the relative amount of each subject to be covered, you can choose suitable study materials. For beginning level jobs, or even advanced ones, if you have a pronounced weakness in some aspect of your training, read a modern, standard textbook in that field. Be sure it is up to date and has general coverage. Such books are normally available at your library, and the librarian will be glad to help you locate one. For entry-level positions, questions of appropriate difficulty are chosen – neither highly advanced questions, nor those too simple. Such questions require careful thought but not advanced training.

If the position for which you are applying is technical or advanced, you will read more advanced, specialized material. If you are already familiar with the basic principles of your field, elementary textbooks would waste your time. Concentrate on advanced textbooks and technical periodicals. Think through the concepts and review difficult problems in your field.

These are all general sources. You can get more ideas on your own initiative, following these leads. For example, training manuals and publications of the government agency which employs workers in your field can be useful, particularly for technical and professional positions. A letter or visit to the government department involved may result in more specific study suggestions, and certainly will provide you with a more definite idea of the exact nature of the position you are seeking.

III. KINDS OF TESTS

Tests are used for purposes other than measuring knowledge and ability to perform specified duties. For some positions, it is equally important to test ability to make adjustments to new situations or to profit from training. In others, basic mental abilities not dependent on information are essential. Questions which test these things may not appear as pertinent to the duties of the position as those which test for knowledge and information. Yet they are often highly important parts of a fair examination. For very general questions, it is almost impossible to help you direct your study efforts. What we can do is to point out some of the more common of these general abilities needed in public service positions and describe some typical questions.

1) General information

Broad, general information has been found useful for predicting job success in some kinds of work. This is tested in a variety of ways, from vocabulary lists to questions about current events. Basic background in some field of work, such as sociology or economics, may be sampled in a group of questions. Often these are principles which have become familiar to most persons through exposure rather than through formal training. It is difficult to advise you how to study for these questions; being alert to the world around you is our best suggestion.

2) Verbal ability

An example of an ability needed in many positions is verbal or language ability. Verbal ability is, in brief, the ability to use and understand words. Vocabulary and grammar tests are typical measures of this ability. Reading comprehension or paragraph interpretation questions are common in many kinds of civil service tests. You are given a paragraph of written material and asked to find its central meaning.

3) Numerical ability

Number skills can be tested by the familiar arithmetic problem, by checking paired lists of numbers to see which are alike and which are different, or by interpreting charts and graphs. In the latter test, a graph may be printed in the test booklet which you are asked to use as the basis for answering questions.

4) Observation

A popular test for law-enforcement positions is the observation test. A picture is shown to you for several minutes, then taken away. Questions about the picture test your ability to observe both details and larger elements.

5) Following directions

In many positions in the public service, the employee must be able to carry out written instructions dependably and accurately. You may be given a chart with several columns, each column listing a variety of information. The questions require you to carry out directions involving the information given in the chart.

6) Skills and aptitudes

Performance tests effectively measure some manual skills and aptitudes. When the skill is one in which you are trained, such as typing or shorthand, you can practice. These tests are often very much like those given in business school or high school courses. For many of the other skills and aptitudes, however, no short-time preparation can be made. Skills and abilities natural to you or that you have developed throughout your lifetime are being tested.

Many of the general questions just described provide all the data needed to answer the questions and ask you to use your reasoning ability to find the answers. Your best preparation for these tests, as well as for tests of facts and ideas, is to be at your physical and mental best. You, no doubt, have your own methods of getting into an exam-taking mood and keeping "in shape." The next section lists some ideas on this subject.

IV. KINDS OF QUESTIONS

Only rarely is the "essay" question, which you answer in narrative form, used in civil service tests. Civil service tests are usually of the short-answer type. Full instructions for answering these questions will be given to you at the examination. But in case this is your first experience with short-answer questions and separate answer sheets, here is what you need to know:

1) Multiple-choice Questions

Most popular of the short-answer questions is the "multiple choice" or "best answer" question. It can be used, for example, to test for factual knowledge, ability to solve problems or judgment in meeting situations found at work.

A multiple-choice question is normally one of three types—
- It can begin with an incomplete statement followed by several possible endings. You are to find the one ending which *best* completes the statement, although some of the others may not be entirely wrong.
- It can also be a complete statement in the form of a question which is answered by choosing one of the statements listed.

- It can be in the form of a problem – again you select the best answer.

Here is an example of a multiple-choice question with a discussion which should give you some clues as to the method for choosing the right answer:

When an employee has a complaint about his assignment, the action which will *best* help him overcome his difficulty is to
  A. discuss his difficulty with his coworkers
  B. take the problem to the head of the organization
  C. take the problem to the person who gave him the assignment
  D. say nothing to anyone about his complaint

In answering this question, you should study each of the choices to find which is best. Consider choice "A" – Certainly an employee may discuss his complaint with fellow employees, but no change or improvement can result, and the complaint remains unresolved. Choice "B" is a poor choice since the head of the organization probably does not know what assignment you have been given, and taking your problem to him is known as "going over the head" of the supervisor. The supervisor, or person who made the assignment, is the person who can clarify it or correct any injustice. Choice "C" is, therefore, correct. To say nothing, as in choice "D," is unwise. Supervisors have and interest in knowing the problems employees are facing, and the employee is seeking a solution to his problem.

2) True/False Questions

The "true/false" or "right/wrong" form of question is sometimes used. Here a complete statement is given. Your job is to decide whether the statement is right or wrong.

SAMPLE: A roaming cell-phone call to a nearby city costs less than a non-roaming call to a distant city.

This statement is wrong, or false, since roaming calls are more expensive.

This is not a complete list of all possible question forms, although most of the others are variations of these common types. You will always get complete directions for answering questions. Be sure you understand *how* to mark your answers – ask questions until you do.

V. RECORDING YOUR ANSWERS

Computer terminals are used more and more today for many different kinds of exams.
For an examination with very few applicants, you may be told to record your answers in the test booklet itself. Separate answer sheets are much more common. If this separate answer sheet is to be scored by machine – and this is often the case – it is highly important that you mark your answers correctly in order to get credit.

An electronic scoring machine is often used in civil service offices because of the speed with which papers can be scored. Machine-scored answer sheets must be marked with a pencil, which will be given to you. This pencil has a high graphite content which responds to the electronic scoring machine. As a matter of fact, stray dots may register as answers, so do not let your pencil rest on the answer sheet while you are pondering the correct answer. Also, if your pencil lead breaks or is otherwise defective, ask for another.

Since the answer sheet will be dropped in a slot in the scoring machine, be careful not to bend the corners or get the paper crumpled.

The answer sheet normally has five vertical columns of numbers, with 30 numbers to a column. These numbers correspond to the question numbers in your test booklet. After each number, going across the page are four or five pairs of dotted lines. These short dotted lines have small letters or numbers above them. The first two pairs may also have a "T" or "F" above the letters. This indicates that the first two pairs only are to be used if the questions are of the true-false type. If the questions are multiple choice, disregard the "T" and "F" and pay attention only to the small letters or numbers.

Answer your questions in the manner of the sample that follows:

32. The largest city in the United States is
    A. Washington, D.C.
    B. New York City
    C. Chicago
    D. Detroit
    E. San Francisco

1) Choose the answer you think is best. (New York City is the largest, so "B" is correct.)
2) Find the row of dotted lines numbered the same as the question you are answering. (Find row number 32)
3) Find the pair of dotted lines corresponding to the answer. (Find the pair of lines under the mark "B.")
4) Make a solid black mark between the dotted lines.

VI. BEFORE THE TEST

Common sense will help you find procedures to follow to get ready for an examination. Too many of us, however, overlook these sensible measures. Indeed, nervousness and fatigue have been found to be the most serious reasons why applicants fail to do their best on civil service tests. Here is a list of reminders:

- Begin your preparation early – Don't wait until the last minute to go scurrying around for books and materials or to find out what the position is all about.
- Prepare continuously – An hour a night for a week is better than an all-night cram session. This has been definitely established. What is more, a night a week for a month will return better dividends than crowding your study into a shorter period of time.
- Locate the place of the exam – You have been sent a notice telling you when and where to report for the examination. If the location is in a different town or otherwise unfamiliar to you, it would be well to inquire the best route and learn something about the building.
- Relax the night before the test – Allow your mind to rest. Do not study at all that night. Plan some mild recreation or diversion; then go to bed early and get a good night's sleep.
- Get up early enough to make a leisurely trip to the place for the test – This way unforeseen events, traffic snarls, unfamiliar buildings, etc. will not upset you.
- Dress comfortably – A written test is not a fashion show. You will be known by number and not by name, so wear something comfortable.

- Leave excess paraphernalia at home – Shopping bags and odd bundles will get in your way. You need bring only the items mentioned in the official notice you received; usually everything you need is provided. Do not bring reference books to the exam. They will only confuse those last minutes and be taken away from you when in the test room.
- Arrive somewhat ahead of time – If because of transportation schedules you must get there very early, bring a newspaper or magazine to take your mind off yourself while waiting.
- Locate the examination room – When you have found the proper room, you will be directed to the seat or part of the room where you will sit. Sometimes you are given a sheet of instructions to read while you are waiting. Do not fill out any forms until you are told to do so; just read them and be prepared.
- Relax and prepare to listen to the instructions
- If you have any physical problem that may keep you from doing your best, be sure to tell the test administrator. If you are sick or in poor health, you really cannot do your best on the exam. You can come back and take the test some other time.

VII. AT THE TEST

The day of the test is here and you have the test booklet in your hand. The temptation to get going is very strong. Caution! There is more to success than knowing the right answers. You must know how to identify your papers and understand variations in the type of short-answer question used in this particular examination. Follow these suggestions for maximum results from your efforts:

1) Cooperate with the monitor

The test administrator has a duty to create a situation in which you can be as much at ease as possible. He will give instructions, tell you when to begin, check to see that you are marking your answer sheet correctly, and so on. He is not there to guard you, although he will see that your competitors do not take unfair advantage. He wants to help you do your best.

2) Listen to all instructions

Don't jump the gun! Wait until you understand all directions. In most civil service tests you get more time than you need to answer the questions. So don't be in a hurry. Read each word of instructions until you clearly understand the meaning. Study the examples, listen to all announcements and follow directions. Ask questions if you do not understand what to do.

3) Identify your papers

Civil service exams are usually identified by number only. You will be assigned a number; you must not put your name on your test papers. Be sure to copy your number correctly. Since more than one exam may be given, copy your exact examination title.

4) Plan your time

Unless you are told that a test is a "speed" or "rate of work" test, speed itself is usually not important. Time enough to answer all the questions will be provided, but this does not mean that you have all day. An overall time limit has been set. Divide the total time (in minutes) by the number of questions to determine the approximate time you have for each question.

5) Do not linger over difficult questions

If you come across a difficult question, mark it with a paper clip (useful to have along) and come back to it when you have been through the booklet. One caution if you do this – be sure to skip a number on your answer sheet as well. Check often to be sure that you have not lost your place and that you are marking in the row numbered the same as the question you are answering.

6) Read the questions

Be sure you know what the question asks! Many capable people are unsuccessful because they failed to *read* the questions correctly.

7) Answer all questions

Unless you have been instructed that a penalty will be deducted for incorrect answers, it is better to guess than to omit a question.

8) Speed tests

It is often better NOT to guess on speed tests. It has been found that on timed tests people are tempted to spend the last few seconds before time is called in marking answers at random – without even reading them – in the hope of picking up a few extra points. To discourage this practice, the instructions may warn you that your score will be "corrected" for guessing. That is, a penalty will be applied. The incorrect answers will be deducted from the correct ones, or some other penalty formula will be used.

9) Review your answers

If you finish before time is called, go back to the questions you guessed or omitted to give them further thought. Review other answers if you have time.

10) Return your test materials

If you are ready to leave before others have finished or time is called, take ALL your materials to the monitor and leave quietly. Never take any test material with you. The monitor can discover whose papers are not complete, and taking a test booklet may be grounds for disqualification.

VIII. EXAMINATION TECHNIQUES

1) Read the general instructions carefully. These are usually printed on the first page of the exam booklet. As a rule, these instructions refer to the timing of the examination; the fact that you should not start work until the signal and must stop work at a signal, etc. If there are any *special* instructions, such as a choice of questions to be answered, make sure that you note this instruction carefully.

2) When you are ready to start work on the examination, that is as soon as the signal has been given, read the instructions to each question booklet, underline any key words or phrases, such as *least*, *best*, *outline*, *describe* and the like. In this way you will tend to answer as requested rather than discover on reviewing your paper that you *listed without describing*, that you selected the *worst* choice rather than the *best* choice, etc.

3) If the examination is of the objective or multiple-choice type – that is, each question will also give a series of possible answers: A, B, C or D, and you are called upon to select the best answer and write the letter next to that answer on your answer paper – it is advisable to start answering each question in turn. There may be anywhere from 50 to 100 such questions in the three or four hours allotted and you can see how much time would be taken if you read through all the questions before beginning to answer any. Furthermore, if you come across a question or group of questions which you know would be difficult to answer, it would undoubtedly affect your handling of all the other questions.

4) If the examination is of the essay type and contains but a few questions, it is a moot point as to whether you should read all the questions before starting to answer any one. Of course, if you are given a choice – say five out of seven and the like – then it is essential to read all the questions so you can eliminate the two that are most difficult. If, however, you are asked to answer all the questions, there may be danger in trying to answer the easiest one first because you may find that you will spend too much time on it. The best technique is to answer the first question, then proceed to the second, etc.

5) Time your answers. Before the exam begins, write down the time it started, then add the time allowed for the examination and write down the time it must be completed, then divide the time available somewhat as follows:
   - If 3-1/2 hours are allowed, that would be 210 minutes. If you have 80 objective-type questions, that would be an average of 2-1/2 minutes per question. Allow yourself no more than 2 minutes per question, or a total of 160 minutes, which will permit about 50 minutes to review.
   - If for the time allotment of 210 minutes there are 7 essay questions to answer, that would average about 30 minutes a question. Give yourself only 25 minutes per question so that you have about 35 minutes to review.

6) The most important instruction is to *read each question* and make sure you know what is wanted. The second most important instruction is to *time yourself properly* so that you answer every question. The third most important instruction is to *answer every question*. Guess if you have to but include something for each question. Remember that you will receive no credit for a blank and will probably receive some credit if you write something in answer to an essay question. If you guess a letter – say "B" for a multiple-choice question – you may have guessed right. If you leave a blank as an answer to a multiple-choice question, the examiners may respect your feelings but it will not add a point to your score. Some exams may penalize you for wrong answers, so in such cases *only*, you may not want to guess unless you have some basis for your answer.

7) Suggestions
   a. Objective-type questions
      1. Examine the question booklet for proper sequence of pages and questions
      2. Read all instructions carefully
      3. Skip any question which seems too difficult; return to it after all other questions have been answered
      4. Apportion your time properly; do not spend too much time on any single question or group of questions

5. Note and underline key words – *all, most, fewest, least, best, worst, same, opposite*, etc.
6. Pay particular attention to negatives
7. Note unusual option, e.g., unduly long, short, complex, different or similar in content to the body of the question
8. Observe the use of "hedging" words – *probably, may, most likely*, etc.
9. Make sure that your answer is put next to the same number as the question
10. Do not second-guess unless you have good reason to believe the second answer is definitely more correct
11. Cross out original answer if you decide another answer is more accurate; do not erase until you are ready to hand your paper in
12. Answer all questions; guess unless instructed otherwise
13. Leave time for review

   b. Essay questions
1. Read each question carefully
2. Determine exactly what is wanted. Underline key words or phrases.
3. Decide on outline or paragraph answer
4. Include many different points and elements unless asked to develop any one or two points or elements
5. Show impartiality by giving pros and cons unless directed to select one side only
6. Make and write down any assumptions you find necessary to answer the questions
7. Watch your English, grammar, punctuation and choice of words
8. Time your answers; don't crowd material

8) Answering the essay question

Most essay questions can be answered by framing the specific response around several key words or ideas. Here are a few such key words or ideas:

M's: manpower, materials, methods, money, management
P's: purpose, program, policy, plan, procedure, practice, problems, pitfalls, personnel, public relations

   a. Six basic steps in handling problems:
1. Preliminary plan and background development
2. Collect information, data and facts
3. Analyze and interpret information, data and facts
4. Analyze and develop solutions as well as make recommendations
5. Prepare report and sell recommendations
6. Install recommendations and follow up effectiveness

   b. Pitfalls to avoid
1. *Taking things for granted* – A statement of the situation does not necessarily imply that each of the elements is necessarily true; for example, a complaint may be invalid and biased so that all that can be taken for granted is that a complaint has been registered

2. *Considering only one side of a situation* – Wherever possible, indicate several alternatives and then point out the reasons you selected the best one
3. *Failing to indicate follow up* – Whenever your answer indicates action on your part, make certain that you will take proper follow-up action to see how successful your recommendations, procedures or actions turn out to be
4. *Taking too long in answering any single question* – Remember to time your answers properly

IX. AFTER THE TEST

Scoring procedures differ in detail among civil service jurisdictions although the general principles are the same. Whether the papers are hand-scored or graded by machine we have described, they are nearly always graded by number. That is, the person who marks the paper knows only the number – never the name – of the applicant. Not until all the papers have been graded will they be matched with names. If other tests, such as training and experience or oral interview ratings have been given, scores will be combined. Different parts of the examination usually have different weights. For example, the written test might count 60 percent of the final grade, and a rating of training and experience 40 percent. In many jurisdictions, veterans will have a certain number of points added to their grades.

After the final grade has been determined, the names are placed in grade order and an eligible list is established. There are various methods for resolving ties between those who get the same final grade – probably the most common is to place first the name of the person whose application was received first. Job offers are made from the eligible list in the order the names appear on it. You will be notified of your grade and your rank as soon as all these computations have been made. This will be done as rapidly as possible.

People who are found to meet the requirements in the announcement are called "eligibles." Their names are put on a list of eligible candidates. An eligible's chances of getting a job depend on how high he stands on this list and how fast agencies are filling jobs from the list.

When a job is to be filled from a list of eligibles, the agency asks for the names of people on the list of eligibles for that job. When the civil service commission receives this request, it sends to the agency the names of the three people highest on this list. Or, if the job to be filled has specialized requirements, the office sends the agency the names of the top three persons who meet these requirements from the general list.

The appointing officer makes a choice from among the three people whose names were sent to him. If the selected person accepts the appointment, the names of the others are put back on the list to be considered for future openings.

That is the rule in hiring from all kinds of eligible lists, whether they are for typist, carpenter, chemist, or something else. For every vacancy, the appointing officer has his choice of any one of the top three eligibles on the list. This explains why the person whose name is on top of the list sometimes does not get an appointment when some of the persons lower on the list do. If the appointing officer chooses the second or third eligible, the No. 1 eligible does not get a job at once, but stays on the list until he is appointed or the list is terminated.

X. HOW TO PASS THE INTERVIEW TEST

The examination for which you applied requires an oral interview test. You have already taken the written test and you are now being called for the interview test – the final part of the formal examination.

You may think that it is not possible to prepare for an interview test and that there are no procedures to follow during an interview. Our purpose is to point out some things you can do in advance that will help you and some good rules to follow and pitfalls to avoid while you are being interviewed.

What is an interview supposed to test?

The written examination is designed to test the technical knowledge and competence of the candidate; the oral is designed to evaluate intangible qualities, not readily measured otherwise, and to establish a list showing the relative fitness of each candidate – as measured against his competitors – for the position sought. Scoring is not on the basis of "right" and "wrong," but on a sliding scale of values ranging from "not passable" to "outstanding." As a matter of fact, it is possible to achieve a relatively low score without a single "incorrect" answer because of evident weakness in the qualities being measured.

Occasionally, an examination may consist entirely of an oral test – either an individual or a group oral. In such cases, information is sought concerning the technical knowledges and abilities of the candidate, since there has been no written examination for this purpose. More commonly, however, an oral test is used to supplement a written examination.

Who conducts interviews?

The composition of oral boards varies among different jurisdictions. In nearly all, a representative of the personnel department serves as chairman. One of the members of the board may be a representative of the department in which the candidate would work. In some cases, "outside experts" are used, and, frequently, a businessman or some other representative of the general public is asked to serve. Labor and management or other special groups may be represented. The aim is to secure the services of experts in the appropriate field.

However the board is composed, it is a good idea (and not at all improper or unethical) to ascertain in advance of the interview who the members are and what groups they represent. When you are introduced to them, you will have some idea of their backgrounds and interests, and at least you will not stutter and stammer over their names.

What should be done before the interview?

While knowledge about the board members is useful and takes some of the surprise element out of the interview, there is other preparation which is more substantive. It *is* possible to prepare for an oral interview – in several ways:

1) Keep a copy of your application and review it carefully before the interview

This may be the only document before the oral board, and the starting point of the interview. Know what education and experience you have listed there, and the sequence and dates of all of it. Sometimes the board will ask you to review the highlights of your experience for them; you should not have to hem and haw doing it.

2) Study the class specification and the examination announcement

Usually, the oral board has one or both of these to guide them. The qualities, characteristics or knowledges required by the position sought are stated in these documents. They offer valuable clues as to the nature of the oral interview. For example, if the job involves supervisory responsibilities, the announcement will usually indicate that knowledge of modern supervisory methods and the qualifications of the candidate as a supervisor will be tested. If so, you can expect such questions, frequently in the form of a hypothetical situation which you are expected to solve. NEVER go into an oral without knowledge of the duties and responsibilities of the job you seek.

3) Think through each qualification required

Try to visualize the kind of questions you would ask if you were a board member. How well could you answer them? Try especially to appraise your own knowledge and background in each area, *measured against the job sought*, and identify any areas in which you are weak. Be critical and realistic – do not flatter yourself.

4) Do some general reading in areas in which you feel you may be weak

For example, if the job involves supervision and your past experience has NOT, some general reading in supervisory methods and practices, particularly in the field of human relations, might be useful. Do NOT study agency procedures or detailed manuals. The oral board will be testing your understanding and capacity, not your memory.

5) Get a good night's sleep and watch your general health and mental attitude

You will want a clear head at the interview. Take care of a cold or any other minor ailment, and of course, no hangovers.

What should be done on the day of the interview?

Now comes the day of the interview itself. Give yourself plenty of time to get there. Plan to arrive somewhat ahead of the scheduled time, particularly if your appointment is in the fore part of the day. If a previous candidate fails to appear, the board might be ready for you a bit early. By early afternoon an oral board is almost invariably behind schedule if there are many candidates, and you may have to wait. Take along a book or magazine to read, or your application to review, but leave any extraneous material in the waiting room when you go in for your interview. In any event, relax and compose yourself.

The matter of dress is important. The board is forming impressions about you – from your experience, your manners, your attitude, and your appearance. Give your personal appearance careful attention. Dress your best, but not your flashiest. Choose conservative, appropriate clothing, and be sure it is immaculate. This is a business interview, and your appearance should indicate that you regard it as such. Besides, being well groomed and properly dressed will help boost your confidence.

Sooner or later, someone will call your name and escort you into the interview room. *This is it.* From here on you are on your own. It is too late for any more preparation. But remember, you asked for this opportunity to prove your fitness, and you are here because your request was granted.

What happens when you go in?

The usual sequence of events will be as follows: The clerk (who is often the board stenographer) will introduce you to the chairman of the oral board, who will introduce you to the other members of the board. Acknowledge the introductions before you sit down. Do not be surprised if you find a microphone facing you or a stenotypist sitting by. Oral interviews are usually recorded in the event of an appeal or other review.

Usually the chairman of the board will open the interview by reviewing the highlights of your education and work experience from your application – primarily for the benefit of the other members of the board, as well as to get the material into the record. Do not interrupt or comment unless there is an error or significant misinterpretation; if that is the case, do not hesitate. But do not quibble about insignificant matters. Also, he will usually ask you some question about your education, experience or your present job – partly to get you to start talking and to establish the interviewing "rapport." He may start the actual questioning, or turn it over to one of the other members. Frequently, each member undertakes the questioning on a particular area, one in which he is perhaps most competent, so you can expect each member to participate in the examination. Because time is limited, you may also expect some rather abrupt switches in the direction the questioning takes, so do not be upset by it. Normally, a board member will not pursue a single line of questioning unless he discovers a particular strength or weakness.

After each member has participated, the chairman will usually ask whether any member has any further questions, then will ask you if you have anything you wish to add. Unless you are expecting this question, it may floor you. Worse, it may start you off on an extended, extemporaneous speech. The board is not usually seeking more information. The question is principally to offer you a last opportunity to present further qualifications or to indicate that you have nothing to add. So, if you feel that a significant qualification or characteristic has been overlooked, it is proper to point it out in a sentence or so. Do not compliment the board on the thoroughness of their examination – they have been sketchy, and you know it. If you wish, merely say, "No thank you, I have nothing further to add." This is a point where you can "talk yourself out" of a good impression or fail to present an important bit of information. Remember, *you close the interview yourself*.

The chairman will then say, "That is all, Mr. _____, thank you." Do not be startled; the interview is over, and quicker than you think. Thank him, gather your belongings and take your leave. Save your sigh of relief for the other side of the door.

How to put your best foot forward

Throughout this entire process, you may feel that the board individually and collectively is trying to pierce your defenses, seek out your hidden weaknesses and embarrass and confuse you. Actually, this is not true. They are obliged to make an appraisal of your qualifications for the job you are seeking, and they want to see you in your best light. Remember, they must interview all candidates and a non-cooperative candidate may become a failure in spite of their best efforts to bring out his qualifications. Here are 15 suggestions that will help you:

1) Be natural – Keep your attitude confident, not cocky

If you are not confident that you can do the job, do not expect the board to be. Do not apologize for your weaknesses, try to bring out your strong points. The board is interested in a positive, not negative, presentation. Cockiness will antagonize any board member and make him wonder if you are covering up a weakness by a false show of strength.

2) Get comfortable, but don't lounge or sprawl

Sit erectly but not stiffly. A careless posture may lead the board to conclude that you are careless in other things, or at least that you are not impressed by the importance of the occasion. Either conclusion is natural, even if incorrect. Do not fuss with your clothing, a pencil or an ashtray. Your hands may occasionally be useful to emphasize a point; do not let them become a point of distraction.

3) Do not wisecrack or make small talk

This is a serious situation, and your attitude should show that you consider it as such. Further, the time of the board is limited – they do not want to waste it, and neither should you.

4) Do not exaggerate your experience or abilities

In the first place, from information in the application or other interviews and sources, the board may know more about you than you think. Secondly, you probably will not get away with it. An experienced board is rather adept at spotting such a situation, so do not take the chance.

5) If you know a board member, do not make a point of it, yet do not hide it

Certainly you are not fooling him, and probably not the other members of the board. Do not try to take advantage of your acquaintanceship – it will probably do you little good.

6) Do not dominate the interview

Let the board do that. They will give you the clues – do not assume that you have to do all the talking. Realize that the board has a number of questions to ask you, and do not try to take up all the interview time by showing off your extensive knowledge of the answer to the first one.

7) Be attentive

You only have 20 minutes or so, and you should keep your attention at its sharpest throughout. When a member is addressing a problem or question to you, give him your undivided attention. Address your reply principally to him, but do not exclude the other board members.

8) Do not interrupt

A board member may be stating a problem for you to analyze. He will ask you a question when the time comes. Let him state the problem, and wait for the question.

9) Make sure you understand the question

Do not try to answer until you are sure what the question is. If it is not clear, restate it in your own words or ask the board member to clarify it for you. However, do not haggle about minor elements.

10) Reply promptly but not hastily

A common entry on oral board rating sheets is "candidate responded readily," or "candidate hesitated in replies." Respond as promptly and quickly as you can, but do not jump to a hasty, ill-considered answer.

11) Do not be peremptory in your answers

A brief answer is proper – but do not fire your answer back. That is a losing game from your point of view. The board member can probably ask questions much faster than you can answer them.

12) Do not try to create the answer you think the board member wants

He is interested in what kind of mind you have and how it works – not in playing games. Furthermore, he can usually spot this practice and will actually grade you down on it.

13) Do not switch sides in your reply merely to agree with a board member

Frequently, a member will take a contrary position merely to draw you out and to see if you are willing and able to defend your point of view. Do not start a debate, yet do not surrender a good position. If a position is worth taking, it is worth defending.

14) Do not be afraid to admit an error in judgment if you are shown to be wrong

The board knows that you are forced to reply without any opportunity for careful consideration. Your answer may be demonstrably wrong. If so, admit it and get on with the interview.

15) Do not dwell at length on your present job

The opening question may relate to your present assignment. Answer the question but do not go into an extended discussion. You are being examined for a *new* job, not your present one. As a matter of fact, try to phrase ALL your answers in terms of the job for which you are being examined.

Basis of Rating

Probably you will forget most of these "do's" and "don'ts" when you walk into the oral interview room. Even remembering them all will not ensure you a passing grade. Perhaps you did not have the qualifications in the first place. But remembering them will help you to put your best foot forward, without treading on the toes of the board members.

Rumor and popular opinion to the contrary notwithstanding, an oral board wants you to make the best appearance possible. They know you are under pressure – but they also want to see how you respond to it as a guide to what your reaction would be under the pressures of the job you seek. They will be influenced by the degree of poise you display, the personal traits you show and the manner in which you respond.

ABOUT THIS BOOK

This book contains tests divided into Examination Sections. Go through each test, answering every question in the margin. We have also attached a sample answer sheet at the back of the book that can be removed and used. At the end of each test look at the answer key and check your answers. On the ones you got wrong, look at the right answer choice and learn. Do not fill in the answers first. Do not memorize the questions and answers, but understand the answer and principles involved. On your test, the questions will likely be different from the samples. Questions are changed and new ones added. If you understand these past questions you should have success with any changes that arise. Tests may consist of several types of questions. We have additional books on each subject should more study be advisable or necessary for you. Finally, the more you study, the better prepared you will be. This book is intended to be the last thing you study before you walk into the examination room. Prior study of relevant texts is also recommended. NLC publishes some of these in our Fundamental Series. Knowledge and good sense are important factors in passing your exam. Good luck also helps. So now study this Passbook, absorb the material contained within and take that knowledge into the examination. Then do your best to pass that exam.

EXAMINATION SECTION

EXAMINATION SECTION
TEST 1

DIRECTIONS: Each question or incomplete statement is followed by several suggested answers or completions. Select the one that BEST answers the question or completes the statement. *PRINT THE LETTER OF THE CORRECT ANSWER IN THE SPACE AT THE RIGHT.*

Questions 1-6.

DIRECTIONS: Questions 1 through 6 are to be answered on the basis of the following information.

The nursing staff on a medical unit meets every week to discuss problem areas they are encountering while giving nursing care. The areas of discussion are (1) the nursing process and (2) emotional needs of clients.

1. The first staff meeting covers the best nursing approach to meet the clients' emotional needs.
   Which basic factor should be determined FIRST by the staff?

   A. Why the clients behave as they do
   B. Which nursing approach has been effective or needs changing
   C. Which clients have symptoms of increased anxiety
   D. What dependent needs of the client the nurse can meet

2. The staff discusses methods of data collection by the nurse.
   Which would be the MOST significant in making a nursing care plan?

   A. The nursing report on the client's problems
   B. The physical/emotional history supplied by the client's family
   C. Reviewing the client's chart
   D. Interviewing the client immediately on admission

3. The staff agrees that the BASIC principle of planning nursing care is to

   A. accept the client as he or she is
   B. meet the client's needs
   C. believe the client will improve
   D. know the client as a person

4. The staff also stresses that, at the initial interview with the client, the nurse should use open-ended questions to collect data.
   Which question would be a good example?

   A. Are there any questions you want to ask?
   B. Tell me something about yourself.
   C. Can you give me any information?
   D. Were you brought to the hospital by your family?

5. The nursing staff discusses evaluation of nursing care. Which evaluation should be identified as a *halo* evaluation? The client('s)

   A. has learned some control
   B. behavior is to demand attention
   C. continues to be negative
   D. care plan has been effective

6. The staff identifies the best time for the nurse to record the observed behavior of a client. That time is

   A. when the behavior has become a problem
   B. at the end of every shift
   C. immediately after contact with the client
   D. after conferring with other staff members

7. Many people with mental disorders have poor self-images, which they need to improve in order to recover.
   All of the following factors contribute to self-image EXCEPT

   A. body image
   B. personally judging others
   C. relationships within the family
   D. interpersonal relationships outside of the family

8. The MOST important feeling for the nurse to convey to the client in order for the client to accept the nurse is one of

   A. respect for the client   B. willingness to help
   C. professional competence   D. no-nonsense demands

9. A patient being treated for an aggressive personality disorder insists that the last time he was in the clinic he was given lithium, which helped him, and he demands that the nurse get him some immediately.
   The nurse's BEST reply to this demand would be:

   A. We never administer drugs to people in your condition
   B. I will go get some for you if you calm down
   C. You don't need lithium
   D. Be patient, and I'll talk to your doctor about whether lithium would be appropriate for you

10. All of the following principles of psychiatric-mental health nursing help form the basis of the therapeutic use of self EXCEPT:

    A. Be aware of your own feelings and responses and maintain objectivity while being aware of your own needs
    B. Accept clients as they are, be nonjudgmental, and recognize that emotions influence behaviors
    C. Use sympathy, not empathy, and observe a client's behaviors to analyze needs and problems
    D. Avoid verbal reprimands, physical force, giving advice, or imposing your own values on clients. Also assess clients in the context of their social and cultural group.

Questions 11-20.

DIRECTIONS: Questions 11 through 20 are to be answered on the basis of the following information.

Pete Jones, the mental health nurse specialist, conducts group therapy sessions for the outpatient clinic.

11. During group formation, Mr. Jones should SPECIFICALLY select a group of clients that is no more than _____ in number and has homogeneity of _____.

    A. 6; goals
    B. 4; age and sex
    C. 14; ability and willingness
    D. 10; problems and needs

12. Mr. Jones has selected his group, and they meet daily from 2 to 3 P.M. It is a closed group and does not allow any interruptions.
    During the period that it takes the group to become acquainted, what kind of behavior would Mr. Jones expect from the group?

    A. Open and positive interaction, rather than projection of their feelings
    B. Conflict, lack of unity, testing, and politeness toward each other
    C. Trust and acceptance of each other and the therapist
    D. Discussion centering on the mental health unit and their expectations

13. Mr. Jones explains to the group that its main function is sharing feelings and behaviors among the members. The group is often a substitute for, or is compared to, one's own family.
    What does the group accomplish for each member through this identification process?
    The group

    A. gives the client hope in himself and makes him realize that others are available for comfort and acceptance
    B. teaches the client new skills in socialization that will be more acceptable to his family
    C. assists the client in replacing negative past experiences with a new set of positive group experiences
    D. helps the client feel that he is being helpful and interested in the well-being of others

14. Mr. Jones' group therapy is based on interventive-exploratory therapy.
    When he defines this type of therapy to his group, what should he say?

    A. You will verbally express your emotional problems with individual and group relationships.
    B. The main focus of this group is the support of existing coping mechanisms.
    C. The emphasis is on social interaction, which encourages control.
    D. This is an intellectual and emotional exchange of things that you value.

15. Mr. Jones observes that one of the clients monopolizes the group discussion. What action should Mr. Jones take?

    A. Accept the client's behavior as his/her way of coping
    B. Allow the group members to intervene if they are able to
    C. Interrupt and ask the client to limit the discussion
    D. Ask another client if this discussion is relevant

16. One of the clients in the group is verbally aggressive toward another client. What should Mr. Jones do INITIALLY?

    A. Set up individual therapy to explore the hostile client's feelings
    B. Ask the aggressive client to leave the group until control is gained
    C. Set an example by being uninvolved with the aggressor
    D. Sit still, observe, and avoid taking sides with either client

17. Mr. Jones and the group feel that they are not progressing. What should the group do?

    A. Explore the reasons for the lack of group productivity
    B. Establish other goals that will be more compatible to the group
    C. Disband because the members are not compatible
    D. Accept new members into the group to provide more feedback

18. After a group session, one of the clients says, *Today I felt we were really a group*. When Mr. Jones asks that client to identify the reason for this feeling, which response demonstrates ACCURATELY that the group was cohesive?

    A. We have learned to speak directly to each other rather than to the whole group.
    B. We have been able to discuss similarities of thoughts and conflicts.
    C. We have not been so hostile or anxious with each other.
    D. As individuals, each one has identified ways of fulfilling his or her goal.

19. During one of the group sessions, Mrs. Elena tells Mr. Jones that he is one of the smartest men she has ever known and feels she has learned so much from him. How should Mr. Jones respond?

    A. That is very nice of you, but we are not here to discuss me.
    B. We are not here to give compliments to any one member.
    C. You seem anxious, share your feelings with us.
    D. The purpose of the group is to learn more about each other.

20. The group has reached its goal and is now talking about termination. Which action by the group members shows that they are ready to terminate the group?

    A. Members no longer feel abandoned, rejected, or forsaken.
    B. Feelings are expressed that members of the group will keep in touch.
    C. Each member learns to handle his or her own feelings of loss without support.
    D. There is effective coping with feelings of loss and separation anxiety.

KEY (CORRECT ANSWERS)

1. C
2. D
3. A
4. B
5. C

6. C
7. B
8. A
9. D
10. C

11. D
12. B
13. C
14. A
15. B

16. D
17. A
18. B
19. C
20. D

TEST 2

DIRECTIONS: Each question or incomplete statement is followed by several suggested answers or completions. Select the one that BEST answers the question or completes the statement. *PRINT THE LETTER OF THE CORRECT ANSWER IN THE SPACE AT THE RIGHT.*

Questions 1-6.

DIRECTIONS: Questions 1 through 6 are to be answered on the basis of the following information.

Ms. Cohen is a nurse working in a crisis center with a volunteer group.

1. One of the volunteers asks, *What is a crisis?* The nurse should reply that a crisis is a situation in which the person or family

    A. is too subjectively involved to realize when there is a problem
    B. constantly looks to others to resolve certain conflicts
    C. has difficulty with growth and development periods
    D. has had no experience in knowing how to deal with a problem

2. Ms. Cohen tells the volunteers that those working with people in crisis should recognize that one of the first reactions to crisis is the use of defense mechanisms. They should know that these defenses at the time of a crisis

    A. are useful in helping clients protect themselves
    B. are irrelevant, as they are part of the basic personality
    C. should be interrupted to prevent further damage
    D. are an indication that the client is coping well

3. Ms. Cohen explains to the group that people in crisis often use isolation as a defense. Ms. Cohen asks, *Which behavior should be assessed as isolation?* The person

    A. blames others for causing the problem
    B. minimizes the seriousness of the problem
    C. accepts the problem intellectually but not emotionally
    D. puts excess energy in another area to neutralize the problem

4. Ms. Cohen instructs the volunteers that when people in crisis first come to the center to seek information about their problem, only specific questions should be answered, with no details given at this time.
Why is this approach taken?

    A. The person may be mentally incompetent and may lose control.
    B. A nurse or doctor should give specific information.
    C. The person may be overwhelmed with excessive information.
    D. The person is not interested in detailed information.

5. Ms. Cohen states that when a person is in crisis, the BEST support group would be

   A. the volunteers in the community
   B. close family and friends understanding the problem
   C. other people who have similar problems
   D. the professional working in the crisis center

6. One of the volunteers asks, *Why is the crisis intervention limited from 1 to 6 weeks?* Ms. Cohen replies that a person can stand the disequilibrium only for a limited time, and during this time will

   A. more likely accept intervention to help with coping
   B. return to a familiar pattern of behavior
   C. require long-term counseling after this period
   D. refuse help from any other support group

Questions 7-11.

DIRECTIONS: Questions 7 through 11 are to be answered on the basis of the following information.

Lauren Oland, age 14, was brought to the crisis center by a policeman. She had been raped by a friend of the family.

7. Which nursing action should have TOP priority?

   A. Explain to her that she will be safe here.
   B. Get a detailed description of the attack.
   C. Have a calm and accepting approach.
   D. Treat her physical wounds.

8. Lauren Oland sobs, *My family will kill me if they find out.* Which response by the nurse would be MOST appropriate?

   A. You are underage so your family will have to be informed.
   B. Your family is your best support at this time.
   C. Don't you think that they would rather kill the man?
   D. Tell me how your family reacts during stressful times.

9. After Lauren calms down and accepts Ms. Cohen, she confides, *I feel so dirty. I will never feel clean again.* How should the nurse reply?

   A. This is a normal feeling after what has happened to you.
   B. Are you saying you feel guilty? Let's talk about that feeling.
   C. I can understand; I would feel the same way.
   D. You shouldn't think of yourself as dirty; it wasn't your fault.

10. Lauren tells the nurse, *I feel like my love life is over. No decent boy will ever look at me again.*
    To help Lauren assess the situation, how should the nurse reply?

    A. I know it is difficult, but you are strong.
    B. You are not to blame so you shouldn't punish yourself.

C. What was your relationship with boys before?
D. You are a pretty girl; you will have many boyfriends.

11. Lauren tells Ms. Cohen that she will not testify against the family friend because then everyone will know about her.
Which reply by the nurse would BEST help Lauren with this plan of action?

    A. How do you think you will feel if you do nothing?
    B. It will be a closed court, so no one will know.
    C. This is difficult, but I'm sure you will make the right choice.
    D. You have an obligation to protect other women from this man.

Questions 12-15.

DIRECTIONS: Questions 12 through 15 are to be answered on the basis of the following information.

Kirt Russel, a volunteer, answers the hotline. The caller, a female, tells Kirt that she plans on killing herself.

12. How should Kirt reply?

    A. Are you alone? Is there someone else that I can talk to?
    B. How do you plan on killing yourself?
    C. You have called the right number to prevent that from happening.
    D. What is your name, address, and telephone number?

13. What is the BEST approach for Kirt to take while talking to the *suicide caller*?

    A. Neutral, not condoning or condemning
    B. Distracting the caller from talking about suicide
    C. One of concern and support
    D. Acting as the conscience of the caller

14. The caller identifies herself as Barbra and states that she is going to poison herself. What should Kirt then say?

    A. Have you thought of the agony of such a death?
    B. What kind of poison are you going to take?
    C. Tell me if you've ever had these feelings before.
    D. Give me the name of your doctor.

15. Kirt keeps Barbra on the phone, pleading with her not to hang up, but to keep talking to him.
Kirt's purpose in doing this is to

    A. give her time to gain her equilibrium and reconsider her actions
    B. let her know that someone cares enough to talk to her
    C. keep her mind off her problems and the thought of suicide
    D. keep her occupied until an emergency team arrives

Questions 16-20.

DIRECTIONS: Questions 16 through 20 are to be answered on the basis of the following information.

Doreen Darby is a 16-year-old high school student with a history of poor social contact. Always an introvert, for the past month Doreen has refused to go to school, spent her time in bed, and taken nourishment only when spoon-fed. Her family took her to the emergency room of the general hospital when she reported that voices had told her she was *no good and should stay away from others.*

16. The nurse in the emergency room identifies Doreen's behavior as depersonalization. This term is BEST described as

    A. pathological narcissism
    B. inability to empathize with others
    C. experiencing the world as dreamlike
    D. absence of a moral code

17. The staff is planning Doreen's immediate care. The MOST suitable choice at this time would be

    A. weekly visits to the psychiatric clinic for medical therapy and psychotherapy
    B. a small psychiatric unit for 24 hour-a-day treatment
    C. attendance at the day hospital and home with her family at night
    D. in her home, with her family, under the supervision of a psychiatrist

18. Doreen is assessed as having low self-esteem. Which characteristic BEST defines this problem?

    A. Social withdrawal
    B. Flat faces
    C. Alienation from self
    D. Feelings of persecution

19. The nursing staff plans an intensive therapeutic approach for Doreen. Such an approach is CRUCIAL for Doreen because

    A. she will be missing her family, which is her primary support group
    B. she is acutely ill and is completely out of contact with reality
    C. the staff must thoroughly evaluate Doreen's physical, social, and emotional condition
    D. it is critical for her to learn to trust those in her environment

20. Doreen has learned to relate to her primary nurse but refuses to get involved in any of the activities with others on the unit.
Which approach by her primary nurse would be the MOST therapeutic for Doreen?

    A. Telling Doreen she is expected at assigned activities
    B. Becoming involved in activities with Doreen
    C. Observing Doreen with others
    D. Waiting until Doreen asks to attend the activities

Questions 21-25.

DIRECTIONS: Questions 21 through 25 are to be answered on the basis of the following information.

Mrs. Agnes Smith comes to the crisis center with her two small daughters, ages 3 and 4. She has numerous contusions on her face and body. She tells the nurse, *I've been beaten by my husband for the last time. I want to leave him but have no place to go. Maybe when he sobers up, I can go back - if he will go on the wagon.*

21. Which analysis by the nurse takes PRIORITY?

    A. Recognize that the client is correct in wanting to leave her husband
    B. Know the effect the problem will have on the client
    C. Use own past experience to help the client understand her problem
    D. Understand the implications of the problem from the client's viewpoint

22. During the assessment period, which question should the nurse ask Mrs. Smith?

    A. Why can't you plan to live with your family?
    B. Does your husband earn enough to support two households?
    C. How often does your husband beat you?
    D. You say you want to go yet stay. Are there any alternatives we can discuss?

23. Mrs. Smith has identified her problem as being too dependent on her husband. What plan would BEST help her resolve this problem?

    A. Learn to have a better self-image
    B. Talk to her husband about her need to be independent
    C. Find a new home for herself and her children
    D. Go to school or get a job

24. The children and Mrs. Smith have made contact with friends and will be temporarily staying with them.
The nurse understands that this is important for the family at this time because

    A. the tension in their own home is too great
    B. in a neutral environment Mrs. Smith can better plan for the future
    C. they will be safer there than in their own home
    D. both the abuser and abused need time apart

25. Mrs. Smith plans to go to group therapy. Which group would be MOST beneficial at this time?

    A. Abusers Anonymous
    B. Family therapy
    C. Parents without partners
    D. Al-Anon

KEY (CORRECT ANSWERS)

1. D
2. A
3. C
4. C
5. B

6. A
7. C
8. D
9. B
10. C

11. A
12. D
13. C
14. B
15. D

16. C
17. B
18. A
19. D
20. B

21. D
22. D
23. A
24. C
25. B

EXAMINATION SECTION
TEST 1

DIRECTIONS: Each question or incomplete statement is followed by several suggested answers or completions. Select the one that BEST answers the question or completes the statement. *PRINT THE LETTER OF THE CORRECT ANSWER IN THE SPACE AT THE RIGHT.*

Questions 1-16.

DIRECTIONS: Questions 1 through 16 are to be answered on the basis of the following information.

Beth Harrison, age 60, has been admitted to the hospital for diagnostic purposes. She complains of a recent loss of energy and appetite, is extremely nervous, and suffers from insomnia.

1. Upon admission, which data would seem to be the MOST significant cause of these symptoms?
   She

   A. is overweight and smokes
   B. has no medical insurance
   C. has been a widow for ten years
   D. has just sold her home

2. Mrs. Harrison repeatedly states, *All my life, I have helped others, but I was never good enough.*
   The nursing staff assesses her behavior as

   A. aggressive - anger turned on self
   B. neurotic - has overwhelming fears
   C. projective - blames others for her problems
   D. withdrawn - having problems trusting others

3. Mrs. Harrison's behavior is a result of conflict during the early stages of development, because the infant/child was

   A. given inconsistent messages by the parents
   B. compelled to master excessive emotional tensions and drives
   C. threatened by the loss of love of significant others
   D. expected to excel to meet parent's need for status

4. The nurse understands that the reason for Mrs. Harrison's behavior is MOST likely due to

   A. overreaction to being alone
   B. years of poor nutrition
   C. grief over a loss
   D. fear of the unknown

5. After the nurse and Mrs. Harrison introduce themselves, which statement by the nurse would be MOST therapeutic?

   A. You will get the best of help here.
   B. Life must be difficult for you.
   C. Why did you come to the hospital?
   D. Tell me about yourself.

6. The nurse and Mrs. Harrison are establishing short-term goals.
   The goal that should be given PRIORITY is that she will be able to

   A. communicate her needs to a professional
   B. practice good nutrition and eating habits
   C. identify who she is and what she wants
   D. identify the relationship between emotion and organic illness

7. The reason the nurse and Mrs. Harrison planned for a priority short-term goal was that

   A. Mrs. Harrison needs immediate nursing intervention
   B. Mrs. Harrison could accomplish it while in the hospital
   C. attainment of all other goals is basic to this goal
   D. it is the only goal that the nurse and Mrs. Harrison can share

8. Mrs. Harrison tells the nurse that she feels unable to concentrate and states, *I'm afraid I will lose all control.*
   Which reply by the nurse would BEST expand the client's experience?

   A. Do you think that you will hurt yourself when you lose control?
   B. What is it that you fear you will lose control of?
   C. Are you afraid that you will become dependent on others?
   D. This must be difficult for you, but I will help you.

9. The nurse understands that Mrs. Harrison's inability to concentrate is due to her high level of anxiety.
   The nursing plan that would BEST help reduce the client's anxiety would be to

   A. provide activities that will distract her from the anxiety
   B. communicate with her based upon her level of anxiety
   C. ignore her anxiety and give praise when she is free of anxiety
   D. teach her techniques to reduce anxiety

10. The nurse understands that problem solving would bedifficult or almost impossible while Mrs. Harrison has difficulty in concentrating.
    Therefore, the MOST important action during the initial phase of the therapeutic interview is for the nurse to

    A. help her feel that she is accepted and understood
    B. teach her exercises that will help improve her concentration
    C. give step-by-step details of the structure of the interview
    D. ask questions that are simple and to the point

11. The nurse recognizes that Mrs. Harrison is ready for the working phase of the therapeutic interview when she tells the nurse:

    A. You have helped me by identifying my problem for me
    B. I know what is wrong with me; I don't like myself
    C. I am feeling less anxious now and can concentrate
    D. There is nothing wrong with me; all my reports were negative

12. Which action by the nurse during the working phase of the interview would be MOST therapeutic?

    A. Giving the client reassurance when she makes a decision
    B. Using silence throughout the working phase
    C. Advising the client what her plan of action should be
    D. Maintaining the focus and helping the client make a plan

13. The BEST long-term goal for Mrs. Harrison would be to return to the community and have

    A. appropriate ways of communicating feelings
    B. a residence in a new neighborhood
    C. improved relationships with others
    D. a feeling that someone cares in the hospital

14. One day Mrs. Harrison states that the doctor told her to join a social group and find other activities outside of her home. She asks the nurse, *Do you think that this will help me when I go home?*
    Which reply by the nurse would be MOST helpful?

    A. You should join a group of your own age and experience.
    B. You never were one to socialize much, were you?
    C. How do you feel that a social group might benefit you?
    D. I think that would be an excellent idea.

15. During the termination phase of the therapeutic interview, after a plan of action has been determined, the nurse should expect which behavior from Mrs. Harrison?

    A. Refusing to talk to the nurse and others on the staff
    B. Making plans to leave the hospital
    C. Telling the nurse she feels worse than on admission
    D. Complaints of mild anxiety and some restlessness

16. The BEST time for the nurse to evaluate Mrs. Harrison's nursing plan is

    A. in the community after she joins a group
    B. in the hospital just before she is discharged
    C. after she has had time to act on the goals
    D. at home immediately after she is discharged

Questions 17-20.

DIRECTIONS: Questions 17 through 20 are to be answered on the basis of the following information.

Leo Johnson has a compound fracture of the temporal bone (basal skull fracture).

17. The nurse notices bleeding from the orifice of the ear. Which action by the nurse can be safely used to determine if the drainage contains cerebrospinal fluid (CSF)?
The nurse should

   A. gently suction the ear and send the specimen to the laboratory
   B. swab the orifice of the ear with a sterile applicator and send the specimen to the laboratory
   C. obtain a negative reading for sugar after testing the CSF with Tes-Tape
   D. blot the drainage with a sterile gauze pad and look for a clear wet ring around the spot of blood

The nursing care plan states, *Observe for early signs of increased intracranial pressure (IIP).*
Early signs of IIP include

   A. rising blood pressure and bradycardia
   B. restlessness and change in level of consciousness
   C. widening pulse pressure and dilated pupils
   D. elevated temperature and decerebrate posturing

19. During the INITIAL period after the head injury, nursing intervention for Mr. Johnson should include

   A. awakening the client every 2 hours to determine his level of consciousness
   B. packing the ears with cotton balls to stop bleeding
   C. administering fluids to replace loss from bleeding
   D. placing the client in semi-Fowler's position to combat shock

20. Before discharge, a computerized axial tomogram will be performed to rule out any intracranial or extracranial bleeding.
Mr. Johnson should be told that

   A. he will experience a burning sensation as the dye is being injected into an arterial catheter
   B. the procedure is noninvasive and he will not feel any pain
   C. local anesthetic is used before injecting air into the ventricles of the brain via the spinal canal
   D. the procedure is done in the operating room under anesthesia

Questions 21-25.

DIRECTIONS: Questions 21 through 25 are to be answered on the basis of the following information.

Mrs. Franklin, 40 years old, has given birth to a girl with Down's syndrome. She is short, has transverse palmer crease, hyperflexibility, and slanted eyelids. The physician tells Mr. and Mrs. Franklin that their daughter will be a slow learner but she should be trainable.

21. When the nurse brings Mrs. Franklin her daughter for the first time, Mrs. Franklin appears reluctant to touch or hold the baby.
 How should the nurse respond?

 A. Put Mrs. Franklin in a comfortable position and place the baby within her reach
 B. Hold the baby for Mrs. Franklin and explain that she does not have to hold her
 C. Tell her she will take the baby away until she is more comfortable
 D. Ask her if she would like to hold her baby and provide her with the opportunity

21.____

22. The nurse is planning care for Mrs. Franklin.
 Which action would assist Mrs. Franklin the MOST in acceptance of her child?

 A. Plan to have another mother who has a child with Down's syndrome visit Mrs. Franklin
 B. Anticipate the baby's needs and provide for them until Mrs. Franklin is able to accept her baby
 C. The mother should handle and touch the baby, and the nurse should teach her about infant care
 D. Explain to Mrs. Franklin that special nursing care must be given to a baby with Down's syndrome

22.____

23. Mr. Franklin asks the nurse what skills his child will be able to accomplish if she is trainable.
 Which response is MOST appropriate?
 The trainable child

 A. will eventually be able to live independently
 B. will be able to take care of her activities of daily living
 C. can find employment if she has some supervision
 D. should be able to learn to read and write

23.____

24. The nurse explains to Mrs. Franklin that her child may need a longer period of *mothering* than her other children because the slow learner

 A. has problems with controlling impulses
 B. has a stronger attachment to the mother
 C. takes longer to develop self-confidence
 D. is satisfied with the status quo

24.____

25. The nurse explains to Mr. and Mrs. Franklin that their daughter, if given the love and support of her family, should eventually develop the ability to attend a special class at school. Going to school may be a period of crisis for her because of the

    A. mother's absence for a prolonged period
    B. teacher's need for order and conformity
    C. school's focus on intelligence
    D. child's exposure to rejection by peers

25.___

KEY (CORRECT ANSWERS)

1.	D	11.	B
2.	A	12.	D
3.	C	13.	A
4.	C	14.	C
5.	D	15.	D
6.	A	16.	C
7.	C	17.	D
8.	B	18.	B
9.	B	19.	A
10.	A	20.	B

21.	D
22.	C
23.	B
24.	C
25.	D

TEST 2

DIRECTIONS: Each question or incomplete statement is followed by several suggested answers or completions. Select the one that BEST answers the question or completes the statement. *PRINT THE LETTER OF THE CORRECT ANSWER IN THE SPACE AT THE RIGHT.*

Questions 1-10.

DIRECTIONS: Questions 1 through 10 are to be answered on the basis of the following information.

One of the clients of a primary nurse in the mental health clinic is Ms. Jill Berman, age 30 years. Ms. Berman was admitted because she had attacked a neighbor with a kitchen knife. She claimed that the neighbor was installing electronic equipment in her home to eavesdrop on her activities.

1. Ms. Berman continues to believe that people are spying on her. She tells the nurse, *I'm not crazy; I don't belong here. My neighbor does.*
   How should the nurse respond?

   A. You are upset now, but you'll feel better in a while.
   B. You are safe in the hospital.
   C. This must be a terrifying experience for you.
   D. Your neighbor did not attack you, did she?

   1.____

2. The nurse understands that Ms. Berman uses projective patterns of behavior as a means of coping because developmentally she

   A. never resolved her symbiotic relationship with her mother
   B. could not meet the extravagant demands made of her
   C. was traumatized by sexual behavior she did not understand
   D. was allowed to give way to her impulses

   2.____

3. The staff members recognize that in the early stages of Ms. Berman's illness, she should be observed PARTICULARLY for

   A. an attempt to leave the hospital
   B. any overt or covert signs of suicide
   C. euphoria and acting-out behavior
   D. insomnia and increased agitation

   3.____

4. Ms. Berman treats everyone on the unit with a superior attitude. She tells the nurse that she is the only sane one and all the other clients are crazy.
   The nurse should respond by

   A. telling Ms. Berman that all the clients on the unit are the same as she is
   B. recognizing the reason for her behavior and accepting it
   C. allowing Ms. Berman to express her feelings and by presenting reality
   D. keeping Ms. Berman away from other clients because she can harm them

   4.____

5. Which statement by Ms. Berman should the nurse take as a cue that the client may harm someone on the unit?

    A. That lady over there is really my neighbor in disguise.
    B. The other people on the unit are very disagreeable to me.
    C. The next time anyone attacks me, I'm going to kill him.
    D. My neighbor and the lady on television are planning to kill me.

6. How can the nurse BEST plan to have the other clients accept Ms. Berman as part of the therapeutic community?

    A. Encourage her to express her feelings to the others on the unit.
    B. Assign Ms. Berman to assist the staff with clerical work.
    C. When there are group activities, give her a leadership role.
    D. Show the other clients that she accepts Ms. Berman.

7. The nursing staff plans a therapeutic approach for Ms. Berman. The staff members should

    A. plan all of her activities so that they are routine and nonstimulating
    B. limit her relations with others because of her aggressiveness
    C. meet her aggressive behavior with calmness and control
    D. set high standards for her because this is what she expects of others

8. Ms. Berman's physician orders chlorpromazine (thorazine) 400 mg orally qid for her. Two days after she starts taking the thorazine, she tells the nurse that she feels dizzy. What should be the nurse's PRIMARY action?

    A. Take her blood pressure
    B. Take her to her room to lie down
    C. Discontinue the thorazine
    D. put her head between her knees

9. Ms. Berman experiences nausea and anorexia after taking thorazine. What action should the nurse take FIRST?

    A. Give the medication with meals and restrict fats and carbohydrates.
    B. Explain that the nausea will diminish with time.
    C. Obtain an order for an antacid and give it with the thorazine.
    D. Have Ms. Berman lie down immediately after taking thorazine.

10. Before she is discharged, Ms. Berman asks the nurse if she should move from the neighborhood because she is afraid of losing control again with her neighbor. How should the nurse respond?

    A. It will be difficult for you, but you should stay in your neighborhood.
    B. It is up to you, but let's discuss the alternatives.
    C. You must make plans to stay away from your neighbor.
    D. I think it is a good idea to move to a neighborhood where you'll be accepted.

Questions 11-18.

DIRECTIONS: Questions 11 through 18 are to be answered on the basis of the following information.

Ms. Sheila Bell, one of the clients of a nurse in the mental health clinic, sits immobile and expressionless. She appears to be out of contact with the immediate environment.

11. How can the nurse BEST show Ms. Bell that she is concerned? 11.____
    By

    A. explaining to Ms. Bell that she will protect her from any harm
    B. giving Ms. Bell passive range-of-motion exercises to prevent contractures
    C. seeking out Ms. Bell at regular intervals and spending time with her
    D. telling Ms. Bell she is expected to participate in activities

12. In assessing Ms. Bell's behavior, the nurse notes that she has regressed back to a period in which her physical, social, and emotional needs must be met by others. 12.____
    What basic plan is ESSENTIAL for the nurse to make for her client?

    A. Give her a satisfying, personal, and trusting relationship
    B. Keep the nursing routine simple and show acceptance of her behavior
    C. Provide a safe custodial environment, free from stress
    D. Offer her opportunities to learn new ways of communicating

13. In working with regressed clients, such as Ms. Bell, the nurse should assume that the client will be 13.____

    A. totally regressed
    B. responsible for her actions
    C. able to comprehend
    D. able to meet basic hygienic needs

14. Ms. Bell sits or stands motionless for long periods of time. 14.____
    At these times, the nurse should

    A. encourage her client to change her position frequently
    B. change her client's position on an hourly basis
    C. plan an activity in which her client can participate
    D. make provisions for her client to rest in bed

15. What should the nurse say to Ms. Bell about her nonverbal behavior? 15.____

    A. If you understand me, just nod your head.
    B. There are times when all of us do not feel like talking.
    C. You will be talking when you feel better.
    D. I can understand that you do not talk because you are anxious.

16. Ms. Bell begins to talk to the nurse. They are meeting daily in planned therapy sessions, but Ms. Bell has missed the last two sessions. 16.____
    What approach should the nurse take?

    A. Continue to seek the client out and show respect for her.
    B. Remind the client that the sessions are important.
    C. Have one of the other nurses meet with the client.
    D. Ask the client if the sessions have been too stressful.

17. One day, Ms. Bell picks up a chair and throws it on the floor. She starts shouting and moving rapidly back and forth.
    What should the nurse do at this time?

    A. Sit with Ms. Bell until she has gained control.
    B. Tell Ms. Bell that she is upsetting others.
    C. Give Ms. Bell her medication to help her gain control.
    D. Take Ms. Bell to her room to calm down.

18. Ms. Bell has now joined others on the unit. She and the nurse talk about terminating their therapeutic sessions.
    When should the nurse start the termination process?

    A. Wait until the client speaks of termination, and then prepare her.
    B. Start well in advance of termination so the client is prepared.
    C. Prepare the client for termination from the very first session.
    D. Tell the client on the last day that the sessions are over.

Questions 19-25.

DIRECTIONS: Questions 19 through 25 are to be answered on the basis of the following information.

Forty-four-year-old Bev Mazza has behaviors that range from deep depression to euphoria. She has just been admitted to the mental health clinic.

19. Bev is demanding, manipulative, and sexually provocative. How can the nurse BEST intervene?

    A. Allow her to freely act out her feelings.
    B. Accept her manipulative behavior.
    C. Set limits on her acting-out behavior.
    D. Try to meet most of her demands.

20. The nurse understands that Bev uses manipulation because

    A. she is angry at not having her way
    B. it decreases her anxiety
    C. it gives her power over others
    D. she has a poor self-image

21. Bev is receiving lithium carbonate (lithane), 600 mg. tid until a therapeutic blood level is reached.
    The nurse should understand that the dosage is then reduced because

    A. lithium that is not used is stored in fat cells
    B. lithium causes sodium retention
    C. the toxicity and serum level are closely related
    D. drug toleration decreases as the disease increases

22. The nurse tells Bev that lithium will help her control her behavior, but that she should report any symptoms of nausea, vomiting, and diarrhea.
The client should also report

   A. an acute anxiety reaction and/or euphoric feeling
   B. shuffling gait and dryness of the mucus membranes
   C. hypotensive or hypertensive feelings
   D. a feeling of drowsiness, muscle weakness, and tremors

23. The nurse should instruct Bev that taking lithium with _____ is contraindicated.

   A. diuretics   B. antibiotics
   C. sedatives   D. tranquilizers

24. What type of social activity should the nurse plan for Bev?

   A. Unit gatherings   B. Table tennis matches
   C. Checkers games   D. Outdoor walks

25. The nurse's predischarge goal for Bev should be to assist her in

   A. making fewer demands on others
   B. having more satisfying experiences
   C. returning to her family and job
   D. learning to control her feelings

KEY (CORRECT ANSWERS)

1. C   11. C
2. B   12. A
3. B   13. C
4. C   14. B
5. A   15. D

6. D   16. A
7. C   17. C
8. D   18. B
9. A   19. C
10. B   20. D

21. C
22. D
23. A
24. D
25. B

EXAMINATION SECTION
TEST 1

DIRECTIONS: Each question or incomplete statement is followed by several suggested answers or completions. Select the one the BEST answers the question or completes the statement. *PRINT THE LETTER OF THE CORRECT ANSWER IN THE SPACE AT THE RIGHT.*

1. An adult client is seeking treatment at a community mental health clinic. For over a year, she has been overwhelmed with a sense of helplessness and feelings of intense fear, and has had difficulty in performing at work. During the intake interview, the client reports she was sexually abused as a child. According to the DSM-IV, the client would MOST likely be diagnosed as having which disorder? 1.____

    A. Major depressive
    B. Dysthymic
    C. Depersonalization
    D. Posttraumatic stress

2. A woman whose child was recently diagnosed with a terminal illness is referred to a hospital social worker. The woman tells the social worker that her child is not ill and will not need to see the doctor again. Which of the following defense mechanisms is represented by the mother's response? 2.____

    A. Rationalization
    B. Denial
    C. Displacement
    D. Intellectualization

3. A client who has received services for several years in a dialysis unit appears for a routine visit. The nurse notices that the client's affect is markedly different from the last visit. After ruling out compliance concerns, the nurse refers the client to the unit social worker. When seeing the social worker, the client seems detached, self-absorbed, and tearful. The social worker should FIRST: 3.____

    A. assess changes in the client's life situation
    B. schedule a family conference
    C. explore the client's concerns about dying
    D. discuss the client's feelings about dialysis

4. During the first appointment at a family agency, a mother is encouraged by the social worker to express her feelings about the recent placement of her child in a residential facility for the developmentally disabled. The client talks at length instead about her physical health problems. The social worker should FIRST: 4.____

    A. take a full developmental history on the child
    B. redirect the mother to the reasons for the child's placement
    C. evaluate the mother's focus on her own needs
    D. listen attentively to the mother as a way of building rapport

25

5. A social worker at a community mental health center is working with a 21-year-old client who has been experiencing a great deal of rejection from family and friends. The rejections followed an admission by the client that she is a lesbian. During the third session the client begins to cry and says *maybe my mom is right. She says all I need to do is find the right man*. After reflecting the client's unhappy feelings, the social worker should NEXT:

    A. use universalization to provide reassurance to the client about the behavior of others in these circumstances
    B. explore the client's psychosocial history to determine the origins of her sexual orientation
    C. encourage the client to spend some time rethinking her sexual orientation before continuing with the *coming out* process
    D. arrange for a family session to assist the client's family in understanding how to best support a gay family member

6. A social worker is asked to assist an elderly client in making alternative living arrangements. In the initial interview, the client repeatedly attempts to discuss past experiences. What is the social worker's MOST appropriate response to the client?

    A. Ignore the references to the past
    B. Facilitate discussion of the recollections
    C. Evaluate the client for dementia
    D. Redirect the focus to the living arrangements

7. A hospital social worker interviews a couple whose infant has recently been hospitalized for cystic fibrosis. The social worker notices that the parents are reluctant to touch the child. Based on this observation, the social worker's FIRST intervention should be to:

    A. have the parents talk about their reactions to the child's illness
    B. refer the couple to an appropriate support group
    C. evaluate the situation for out-of-home placement for the child
    D. provide the couple with information about cystic fibrosis

8. A client, diagnosed as borderline personality disorder, is verbalizing destructive thoughts directed at herself. While she does admit to depression, she denies any intention to act on the thoughts. The social worker should FIRST:

    A. seek in-patient hospitalization of the client
    B. explore with the client the basis of the depression
    C. complete a suicide risk assessment
    D. refer the client to a psychiatrist for medication

9. As part of the social work process, assessment is BEST described as a:

    A. discrete task to be completed before effective intervention can begin
    B. continuing process throughout the course of intervention
    C. way to measure the effectiveness of the intervention process
    D. method of setting the goals of the intervention process

10. Random error is assessed by:

    A. instrument reliability
    B. instrument validity
    C. external validity
    D. correlation

11. An 50-year-old client diagnosed with chronic alcoholism is at greatest risk for which of the following disorders?

    A. Parkinson's disease
    B. Alzheimer's disease
    C. Korsikoff's disease
    D. Senile dementia

12. A hospital social worker meets with three adult children of an elderly woman. The woman's physician has recommended discharge to a long-term care facility because she is unable to care for herself. The woman refuses this recommendation, and the children cannot agree on a plan. The social worker should FIRST:

    A. define the problem with the children
    B. develop a contract with the woman
    C. gather a social history from the children
    D. provide referrals to home care agencies

13. An adult client who is HIV positive and addicted to drugs and alcohol is receiving social work services from a local AIDS service organization. The client has responsibility for a young grandchild whose mother died of AIDS. The social worker suspects the child is the target of verbal abuse and possible neglect. Which assessment tool can BEST be used by the social worker to gain a better understanding of the situation?

    A. Genogram
    B. Sociogram
    C. Social network map
    D. Ecomap

14. A social worker employed with a public school system makes an initial home visit with a 15-year-old female client at the request of the client's probation officer. Before the social worker begins the assessment of the client and home situation, the client says *I don't have to tell you anything, and I won't tell you anything.* To facilitate the client's participation, the social worker's BEST response would be to tell her that:

    A. there are potential legal consequences for noncompliance
    B. she does indeed control whether she will cooperate
    C. her probation officer has requested the assessment
    D. the assessment is necessary in order to provide services

15. A social worker is interviewing the parents of an adolescent who has recently begun resisting their authority. The parents are angry and confused about how to handle the situation. When the social worker asks questions about other family members, the father says *You're not getting it; it is our son who is the problem.* The social worker should FIRST:

    A. recommend an individual assessment of the adolescent
    B. obtain a developmental history of the adolescent
    C. discuss the importance of understanding everyone's perspective
    D. redirect questions toward the adolescent's behavior

16. During the first interview in the home with a pregnant, unmarried 15-year-old and her mother, the teenager states firmly to the social worker that she wants to keep her baby. The mother asks the social worker to tell the daughter about how difficult it will be to care for the baby. The teenager states, *I don't want to be talked out of keeping my child*. The social worker's FIRST response should be to:

    A. provide the teenager with the positives and negatives of caring for an infant
    B. explore the mother's feelings about her daughter's pregnancy
    C. discuss the teenager's feelings about being forced into a decision
    D. facilitate communication between the mother and daughter

17. Which situation is an example of role reversal in a parent-child relationship?

    A. A seven-year-old girl repeatedly comforting and reassuring her distressed mother following a marital separation
    B. A nine-year-old girl sharing her mother's concerns about household bills
    C. A single mother expecting her 10-year-old son to stay at home unsupervised
    D. An 11-year-old boy demanding of his mother that his meals be on the table at a certain time and that his laundry be done

18. A client is concluding treatment at a family counseling agency. The client feels very appreciative of the social worker's services. At the end of the interview, the client offers a substantial monetary gift to the social worker in addition to paying the fee to the agency. The social worker should:

    A. accept the gift, acknowledging the client's contribution to treatment
    B. refuse the gift, basing the action on ethical standards of practice
    C. accept the money but with the understanding that it will be donated to a local charity
    D. refuse the personal gift and suggest that the client make a donation to the agency instead

19. During group therapy sessions, one of the members continuously blames others in the group for the depression and hopelessness the member experiences. In an effort to address the client's concerns, the social worker should FIRST:

    A. tell the client that these feelings stem from fears
    B. encourage the client to talk about feelings within the group
    C. reiterate the guidelines for the group process
    D. encourage the group to be more sensitive to the client's feelings

20. A child welfare worker is interviewing a parent who admits brutally abusing a child during a rage. On hearing the details, the social worker becomes very angry. To appropriately deal with the anger, the social worker should:

    A. acknowledge the anger to the parent and continue the interview
    B. ignore the anger and proceed with the interview
    C. recognize the anger and discuss it later with the supervisor
    D. request the case be transferred to another social worker

21. A false, fixed belief that is inconsistent with the intelligence and cultural background of the person holding the belief and held despite rational explanation and evidence to the contrary is BEST defined as a(n):

    A. denial
    B. illusion
    C. hallucination
    D. delusion

22. A social worker learns that a father becomes angry when his two-year-old son soils or wets his pants. The father's usual response to this behavior is to yell at the child to *grow up*. The father's behavior MOST likely reflects:

    A. dysfunctional relationship with the child
    B. a distorted perception of child development
    C. a need for developing new ways to cope with stress
    D. displacement of anger toward the other parent

23. In which instance is identifying information from an individual client's case record NOT appropriate for use?

    A. When the social worker is going on vacation, leaving another social worker in charge of the case
    B. When consulting with a professional to gain insight into the client's condition
    C. When agency data is being used for supporting grant proposals
    D. When the social worker is participating in clinical supervision

24. A woman in treatment with a social worker comments that whenever her adolescent son becomes angry, she feels as though she is a failure as a parent. The social worker comments that all adolescents become angry at times. The social worker's technique is known as:

    A. clarifying
    B. interpreting
    C. confronting
    D. normalizing

25. A new supervisor recently promoted from another part of the agency supervises a social worker who conducts group therapy with adolescent clients. In the new position, the supervisor often *drops in* on group sessions and interacts with clients. What is the FIRST step the social worker should take in dealing with this situation?

    A. Integrate the supervisor into group activities with the clients
    B. Talk with the supervisor about the impact of dropping in on groups
    C. Arrange a meeting with the agency director to clarify the supervisor's role
    D. Respect the supervisor's position and allow the supervisor to judge the situation

KEY (CORRECT ANSWERS)

1.	D	11.	C
2.	B	12.	A
3.	A	13.	D
4.	D	14.	B
5.	A	15.	C
6.	B	16.	C
7.	A	17.	A
8.	C	18.	B
9.	B	19.	B
10.	A	20.	C
21.	D		
22.	B		
23.	C		
24.	D		
25.	B		

TEST 2

DIRECTIONS: Each question or incomplete statement is followed by several suggested answers or completions. Select the one the BEST answers the question or completes the statement. *PRINT THE LETTER OF THE CORRECT ANSWER IN THE SPACE AT THE RIGHT.*

1. A client who has completed treatment and resolved the targeted problem is making excessive telephone calls to the social worker. The social worker should:

    A. inform the client that the therapeutic relationship is finished
    B. refer the client to another social worker in the agency
    C. limit the number of calls the social worker will accept
    D. schedule a session to determine any current problems

    1.____

2. In preparing a discharge summary, a social worker writes a case history describing the events leading up to the client's recent hospitalization. The history describes the assessment that was made and the exact symptoms that supported the assessment. The discharge summary was then placed in the client's record. The social worker's supervisor would consider this summary to be:

    A. incomplete because it did not describe what happened in treatment
    B. accurate in giving a complete account supporting admission
    C. satisfactory as a summary for use upon the client's readmission
    D. inappropriate because it contains the assessment

    2.____

3. A client states to a social worker that the social worker reminds him of his former fiancee and that he very much appreciates the social worker's caring for him. This is an example of:

    A. reaction formation
    B. idealization
    C. transference
    D. unconditional positive regard

    3.____

4. A client who is in therapy with a social worker has made significant progress over a period of three months. The client misses a scheduled appointment and does not return the social worker's calls. This behavior is MOST likely an indication of the client's:

    A. misunderstanding of the treatment contract
    B. negative transference in the therapeutic process
    C. establishment of satisfying relationships
    D. readiness for termination of treatment

    4.____

5. In an enmeshed family the children are LEAST likely to exhibit:

    A. role ambiguity
    B. respect for authority
    C. unclear boundaries
    D. difficulty in focusing

    5.____

6. A t-test is used to determine:

   A. causality
   B. standard deviation
   C. significance of differences between sample means
   D. significance at the .05 level of probability

7. A budgeting approach which categorizes expenditures and resources according to the agency's service areas is:

   A. zero-based
   B. program-based
   C. cost benefit
   D. line item

8. A married couple bring their six-year-old son in to see a social worker in private practice. The parents indicate the child recently began bedwetting after being toilet trained for three years. Upon questioning, the parents reveal the bedwetting began shortly after the parents brought their new baby home from the hospital. The six-year-old is MOST likely using the defense mechanism of:

   A. repression
   B. regression
   C. reaction formation
   D. displacement

9. A social worker may limit a client's right to self-determination when:

   A. agency policy requires the social worker to develop treatment plans that minimize liability for the agency
   B. in the social worker's professional opinion the client has made poor choices regarding treatment options
   C. there is pending legal action which would curtail the rights of the client to make decisions
   D. the client's actions or potential actions pose a serious and imminent risk to self or others

10. A social worker wants to develop insight into the ways the social worker's own attitudes and feelings affect relationships with clients. This understanding can be MOST effectively facilitated by a supervisor who promotes the use of:

    A. reflection
    B. analysis
    C. peer review
    D. problem assessment

11. At times a social worker may choose to use closed-ended questions to:

    A. permit the client to be in control
    B. provide needed structure and direction
    C. check out the client's ability to take the initiative
    D. challenge the client's point of view

12. A social worker who has mental health difficulties which interfere with professional judgment and performance should:

    A. continue to practice and engage in all regular activities but safeguard clients
    B. make a self-report on the situation to the state social work licensing board
    C. seek consultation and remedial action, which may include obtaining therapy and adjusting workloads
    D. continue to practice and use appropriate self-disclosure to assist clients to understand similar issues

13. To enhance a client's capacity to make decisions, the social worker should:

    A. analyze the situation for the client
    B. give the client written materials on decision making
    C. ask the client to make a decision independent of the social worker
    D. teach the client how to examine alternate solutions

14. A husband and wife both express to a social worker that their needs are not being met by the other. This situation described by the couple is BEST characterized by the absence of:

    A. boundaries
    B. homeostasis
    C. complementarity
    D. entropy

15. A mother, father, and 16-year-old daughter come to a social worker because the daughter is breaking curfew, running away from home, and failing in school. The mother states at the initial session that she does not know what to do and that they need help. After acknowledging the family's distress, the social worker should:

    A. establish the number of sessions the family is allowed with the social worker
    B. formulate goals for the family members
    C. clarify the parents' expectations of the social work intervention
    D. contract with the adolescent on specific behavior goals

16. A social worker is allowed to violate confidentiality if a client:

    A. initiates a lawsuit against the social worker
    B. is under the age of eighteen
    C. resides in a nursing home
    D. resists recommended social work intervention

17. A social worker faced with a practice situation that may pose an ethical dilemma should FIRST consult the:

    A. current supervisor
    B. social work licensing board'
    C. professional code of ethics
    D. most experienced colleague

18. Crisis intervention is a strategy which generally involves:

    A. having clients face their problems directly and come to terms with them
    B. acting on behalf of clients who cannot act for their own safety
    C. using chaining and sloping to change behaviors
    D. encouraging a high level of intensive activity by the client

19. When faced by a hostile client in an agency setting, it is BEST for the social worker to:

    A. suggest that the client's attitude is making the situation worse
    B. accept the client's hostility and redirect toward nonthreatening topics
    C. set limitations and structure for the interview session
    D. acknowledge the client's feelings and encourage discussion of them

20. If a client has a mood disorder that can be addressed within a limited time frame, the treatment approach of choice is:

    A. cognitive behavioral therapy
    B. crisis intervention
    C. insight-oriented psychotherapy
    D. client-centered therapy

21. A social worker is using a task-centered approach to provide services to a client. After completing an assessment on the client, the social worker's NEXT step should be to:

    A. develop a set of goals with the client
    B. redefine the relationship with the client
    C. outline tasks for the client
    D. monitor the client's progress in goal accomplishment

22. In therapy, a client describes herself as a failure because of repeated publisher rejections of her work. Although the client has a well-paying job and satisfying interpersonal relationships, she defines her identity in terms of her writing. In response to the woman's self-description, the social worker should FIRST:

    A. help the client be more realistic about her abilities
    B. determine if she uses writing to avoid other areas of her life
    C. encourage the client to find other outside interests
    D. further explore the client's feelings about being published

23. During an initial session with a social worker at a community mental health center, a self-referred adult client states, *I just need to let you know, I don't much like social workers*: The client adds that social workers *don't ever seem to be able to help anyone*. In order to facilitate the therapeutic process in this situation, the social worker should:

    A. point out to the client the discrepancy between the desire for services and the dislike of social workers
    B. reassure the client that it is safe to discuss any and all issues, problems, and concerns
    C. acknowledge that the client may have had bad experiences with social workers in the past
    D. encourage the client to explain how the stated view of social workers developed

24. A social worker conducts a home visit to a 45-year-old Latino client whose young son was killed in a recent automobile accident. The social worker observes that a large altar has been made, which contains many candles as well as pictures of the boy and other deceased relatives. The client sobs throughout the interview and tells the social worker that the boy has been communicating to the client nightly through angels. In order to most effectively work with the client, the social worker should FIRST:

    A. refer the client for a medical evaluation
    B. assess the client for psychotic symptoms
    C. explore mourning rituals of the client's family
    D. evaluate the potential of self-harm

25. A social worker is conducting an initial interview with a father and three teenage children. The mother died recently after a lengthy illness. Exploration indicates that the family members were not able to appropriately mourn the mother's death. To help them cope with the unresolved grief, the social worker should FIRST:

    A. encourage the family to discuss their loss
    B. obtain information about the mother's illness
    C. refer the family to a grief support group
    D. engage the family in structural family therapy

KEY (CORRECT ANSWERS)

1. D		11. B	
2. A		12. C	
3. C		13. D	
4. D		14. C	
5. B		15. C	
6. C		16. A	
7. B		17. C	
8. B		18. B	
9. D		19. D	
10. A		20. A	

21. A
22. D
23. D
24. C
25. A

EXAMINATION SECTION
TEST 1

DIRECTIONS: Each question or incomplete statement is followed by several suggested answers or completions. Select the one that BEST answers the question or completes the statement. *PRINT THE LETTER OF THE CORRECT ANSWER IN THE SPACE AT THE RIGHT.*

1. An engaged couple is seeing a social worker for premarital counseling. The woman reports that her fiance's family doesn't accept her because of her religion, and she doesn't want to convert. Her fiance agrees that this is a problem and that he is "torn" between his parents and his wife-to-be. The social worker should **FIRST**:

    A. discuss ways the couple can help his parents accept their relationship
    B. explore the impact of this issue on their relationship
    C. focus on how they plan to handle their religious differences when they are married
    D. recommend individual sessions for each to deal with their feelings

    1.____

2. A single parent of two small children is being seen for an intake interview at a family service agency. She begins to cry when describing her pressures and stresses, and the decisions she is facing since the sudden death of her husband three months ago. She apologizes to the worker for "acting like a baby" and says she knows that her problems could be worse. The social worker should **FIRST**:

    A. suggest that the client prioritize her problems
    B. help the client identify her coping mechanisms
    C. suggest a referral to a bereavement group
    D. acknowledge the difficulty of dealing with numerous problems

    2.____

3. Which of the following factors is **NOT** used in establishing a diagnosis using the DSM-IV?

    A. Physical functioning
    B. Psychosocial stressors
    C. Clinical syndromes
    D. Medical conditions

    3.____

4. A couple in their mid-thirties seek marital counseling from a social worker because they have been experiencing conflict over their sexual relationship. The wife reports that she feels emotionally detached from her husband. They decided early in their marriage not to have children, and both are involved and committed to their careers. The social worker should focus on the couple's:

    A. career objectives
    B. parenting decision
    C. sexual relationship
    D. relationship issues

    4.____

5. A couple comes to a family service agency requesting help in communicating better with each other. The social worker should **FIRST**:

    5.____

37

A. engage the couple in a discussion of male/female communication patterns
B. facilitate role-playing of effective and dysfunctional communication techniques
C. explore what the couple means by better communication
D. gather psychosocial background information on each client, including marital history

6. Which of the following statements is **NOT** true when a social work agency employs a consultant?

    A. The consultant's role need not be sanctioned by the agency's administration.
    B. The consultant's role rests primarily on specialized knowledge and skill.
    C. Consultation is an indirect means of influencing skills of agency staff.
    D. The ultimate beneficiary of consultation is the agency clientele.

7. When a client's behavior is particularly resistant to extinction, the behavior is likely to have been maintained in the past by:

    A. consistent reinforcement
    B. consistent punishment
    C. intermittent reinforcement
    D. intermittent punishment

8. According to the DSM-IV, which of the following symptoms is **NOT** associated with a diagnosis of schizophrenia?

    A. Delusions
    B. Flight of ideas
    C. Affectional flattening
    D. Disorganized speech

9. A six-year-old exhibits repetitive whole-body movements, gross deficits in language development, and a lack of emotional responsiveness. The social worker suspects a diagnosis of:

    A. post-traumatic stress disorder
    B. organic brain syndrome
    C. attention-deficit/hyperactivity disorder
    D. autistic disorder

10. To attempt to extinguish a child's talking to himself in class, a social worker using a behavior modification approach will **FIRST**:

    A. determine how frequently the child talks to himself in class
    B. meet with the child individually and ask to whom he is talking
    C. include the child in a group for children with delayed social skills
    D. remove the child from the class each time he begins talking to himself

11. A client is being seen for symptoms of depression and anxiety, but has been resistant to efforts to refer her for a medication evaluation. The client states that medication is a "crutch" and she should be able to solve her problems without it. During a session following a very upsetting weekend, the client cries and says that she will see "a shrink for pills that will solve her problems." In facilitating the client's referral to the psychiatrist, the social worker should **FIRST**:

A. give the client a list of recommended psychiatrists
B. phone for a psychiatric appointment while the client is still in the office
C. discuss the client's expectation of the consultation
D. suggest the client review her insurance coverage

12. A mother has been referred to a family service agency after learning that her 14-year-old son is diabetic, because of the son's denial of the illness by "forgetting" to test his blood sugar and take insulin as directed. When she asks him how he is feeling, he tells her either to leave him alone or "chill out." The mother bursts into tears, saying she is a "nervous wreck," and worries about her son constantly. The social worker should FIRST:

    A. reassure the mother that her son's reactions are typical adolescent responses
    B. explore family and community resources available to the mother
    C. acknowledge the mother's feelings of fear and apprehension
    D. suggest that a joint interview with mother and son be scheduled

13. The MOST difficult aspect of conducting a cost-benefit analysis is:

    A. determining the units of services
    B. enumerating interventions
    C. establishing a control group
    D. operationally defining outcomes

14. Which of the following statistical tests is a nonparametric test of significance?

    A. Analysis of variance
    B. T-test
    C. Pearson's r
    D. Chi-square

15. A social work manager in a hospital setting decides to establish an interdisciplinary collaborative team to review advanced directive procedures. The FIRST step in this process is to:

    A. identify the areas of expertise needed on the team
    B. identify the persons to be assigned to the team
    C. select the leader of the proposed team
    D. develop a rationale for the inclusion of a social worker

16. The desire for control and perfection is characteristic of which of the following personality disorders?

    A. Borderline
    B. Narcissistic
    C. Obsessive-compulsive
    D. Antisocial

17. After four months of treatment, a client informs his social worker that he has received a job transfer to another city and will move the following week. The social worker should FIRST:

A. review with the client progress made and treatment goals not yet achieved
B. discuss with the client his reasons for not informing the social worker of his plans to move sooner
C. ask the client to sign a release of information form in case he wants to enter treatment at a later time
D. advise the client to become involved in treatment as soon as possible in the new city

18. A social work staff is experiencing an increasing number of clients who fail to keep their appointments. All of the following administrative interventions are appropriate **EXCEPT**:

    A. scheduling a meeting with the staff members to assess their views of the problem
    B. sending a questionnaire to all of the clients who have failed to keep their appointments over the last month
    C. informing clients that they will be charged for not canceling appointments they are unable to keep
    D. terminating clients who do not keep their appointments

19. A five-year-old is scheduled for open heart surgery. Part of the procedure for the operation involves catheterization and an incision in the child's groin. The procedure has been explained to him. He responded to the idea of heart surgery with little or no anxiety but has extreme concern about the catheterization. From a psychodynamic point of view, his anxiety stems from fear of:

    A. mutilation
    B. separation
    C. annihilation
    D. pain

20. A man was referred by his attorney to a social worker after he was charged with sexually molesting a minor. The case is scheduled for trial. The goal of the social worker in treating this client should be to:

    A. gather information in order to prepare a report for the court
    B. determine whether the charge against the client is valid
    C. assist the client in examining his involvement in the charges against him
    D. assist the attorney in preparing the client for his trial

21. A new client has an argument with the agency receptionist before her initial meeting with the social worker. Upon entering the office, the client says to the social worker, in an angry tone, "Why are you looking at me like that?" This remark is an example of which of the following defense mechanisms?

    A. Displacement
    B. Projection
    C. Reaction formation
    D. Sublimation

22. An adult client, arrested for exposing himself, reports that he was urinating after excessive drinking. This is his third arrest for the same offense. He is depressed, anxious, and markedly distressed by his behavior. This client is **BEST** described by which of the following DSM-IV diagnostic categories?

A. Narcissistic personality disorder
B. Gender identity disorder
C. Exhibitionism
D. Alcohol dependence

23. A woman is referred to a hospital social worker by the emergency room physician, who states that the woman must be admitted to the hospital immediately. The woman tells the social worker that she moved to the community only last month and does not have family or friends who can care for her two preschool children during her hospitalization. The social worker's primary responsibility in this situation is to:

    A. secure emergency financial assistance for the woman so that she can pay for the necessary child care
    B. ask the physician to delay the hospitalization until appropriate child care arrangements are made
    C. find a close relative of the children to care for them as soon as possible
    D. assist the client in arranging a temporary placement for the children

24. A social worker tells his supervisor that he is very uncomfortable and anxious when seeing a client described as "intimidating" and "bullying" to others. The social worker expresses feelings of frustration, saying that nothing he says or does seems to work for the client. Initially, the supervisor's **MOST** helpful approach would be to:

    A. observe the next interview through a two-way mirror
    B. recommend that the next session with the client be taped
    C. role-play the situation with the social worker
    D. suggest appropriate reading materials

25. A manic episode includes all of the following characteristics **EXCEPT**:

    A. distractibility
    B. depersonalization
    C. change in sleep pattern
    D. increased involvement in pleasurable activities

KEY (CORRECT ANSWERS)

1. B
2. D
3. A
4. D
5. C
6. A
7. C
8. B
9. D
10. A

11. C
12. C
13. D
14. D
15. A
16. C
17. A
18. D
19. A
20. C

21. B
22. C
23. D
24. C
25. B

TEST 2

DIRECTIONS: Each question or incomplete statement is followed by several suggested answers or completions. Select the one that BEST answers the question or completes the statement. *PRINT THE LETTER OF THE CORRECT ANSWER IN THE SPACE AT THE RIGHT.*

1. The Draw-a-Person test provides diagnostic information about the client's: 1.____

    A. personality structure
    B. eye-motor coordination
    C. thought processes
    D. self-image

2. According to psychoanalytic theory, which of the following is associated with the development of neurosis?   2.____

    A. Interpersonal struggle
    B. Emotion
    C. Impulsivity
    D. Individuation

3. In working with an African-American family, it is MOST important for the social worker to: 3.____

    A. acknowledge possible differences in ethnic background early in the relationship
    B. provide directions and instructions to effect a change in the family's negotiation with social institutions
    C. encourage contact with the extended family as a source of material and emotional support
    D. establish contact with members of the family's church to assure them a social support system

4. A social worker has seen a family for four months, with the initial focus on the youngest child's school attendance problems. During the last two months, the child has been absent from school only once. In the last session of the planned termination, the mother reported that she was to be admitted to the hospital for surgery the following week. The social worker's BEST course of action is to: 4.____

    A. refer the family to a hospital social worker when the mother is admitted
    B. reevaluate with the family the decision to terminate
    C. discontinue treatment, arranging a session when the mother is again able to attend
    D. proceed with plans for the termination of family treatment

5. During an initial session with a social worker, the client describes herself as a very "private person" who doesn't like to talk about herself. She expresses deep concern and anxiety about confidentially and asks the social worker whether "everything I tell you will remain private, and just between us?" The social worker should FIRST: 5.____

    A. explore the basis of the client's anxiety about confidentiality
    B. discuss the difference between self-disclosure and confidentiality
    C. comment on the client's focus on the confidentiality issue
    D. discuss with the client the limits on confidentiality

6. A social worker in a regional social advocacy organization is requested by citizens in an economically depressed rural area to help improve the area's social and economic condition. Recent growth in a nearby urban area has begun to stir citizens' excitement over new employment opportunities as well as fear over unwanted encroachment. The **MOST** appropriate initial strategy for the social worker to employ with the citizen group is to:

    A. educate group members regarding political strategies for gaining power
    B. assess and document the range of services and needs in the community
    C. orient the citizen group to ways they can collect and analyze community data
    D. facilitate problem-solving and communication skills within the community

7. A couple seeks conjoint therapy from a social worker. After an initial assessment, the social worker's **MOST** appropriate intervention is to:

    A. arrange separate sessions for each client to openly express feelings about the other
    B. foster direct communication with the couple in joint sessions
    C. complete a social and developmental history for each partner
    D. encourage both partners to confront the other with areas of marital dissatisfaction

8. In an initial session, which of the following approaches is **LEAST** effective in reducing a client's hesitation to engage in the social worker-client relationship?

    A. Acknowledging the difficulty the client may have in sharing information
    B. Asking directly whether the client is willing to cooperate
    C. Providing the client with information about the number of sessions, their length, and the costs involved
    D. Developing a written contract with the client based on specific outcomes

9. A 14-year-old who has been in treatment with a social worker for the past year has a history of impulsive acting-out behavior. The adolescent is becoming increasingly depressed and is talking about suicide. The social worker should **FIRST**:

    A. request that the family monitor the client's acting-out behaviors
    B. refer the client to a physician for antidepressant medication
    C. intensify the exploration of origin and nature of the depression
    D. assess the client's potential for self-harm

10. In providing feedback to social workers, the supervisor should include all of the following comments about performance **EXCEPT**:

    A. noting how the social worker's performance mirrors the supervisor's expectation
    B. commending the social worker on a specific action
    C. publicly remarking on the positive performance of a social worker
    D. pointing out inappropriate work performance when it occurs

11. A 16-year-old who has been hospitalized frequently for control of diabetes was referred to the hospital social worker. Information about the youth's family indicates that the father is an alcoholic, and the parents experience a great deal of marital discord, arguing frequently in front of the youth. The social worker should **FIRST**:

    A. work with the family concerning the father's alcoholism
    B. refer the parents for marital therapy
    C. explore the youth's experiences in living with a chronic illness

D. discuss the youth's feelings about separation from the family during hospitalizations

12. During a first interview, a client informs a social worker that she engaged in sexual activity with her previous social worker. The sexual involvement began a year after the client began treatment and ended when she decided to terminate treatment against the social worker's advice. Which of the following actions should the social worker take?

    A. Contact the previous social worker, confronting him with the client's information.
    B. Consult the state social work regulatory law regarding reporting requirements
    C. Investigate whether the client's allegations about the former social worker are true
    D. Take no action since the sexual involvement took place outside the therapy sessions

13. A client with a history of impulsive, aggressive behaviors, has been seeing a social worker for three months. During a session, he becomes angry with the social worker and storms out. He cancels his next appointment and sends a letter demanding that his records be released to him immediately, or he will take legal action. He adds that he is seeing a new therapist and has no plans to return to see the social worker. The social worker believes that releasing the record to the client will cause him serious harm. According to professional ethics, the social worker should **FIRST**:

    A. document in the file both the client's request for the record and the rationale for withholding it
    B. seek legal consultation regarding the threat to sue
    C. send the record to the client as requested
    D. alert the social worker's malpractice carrier that a suit might be filed

14. Viewing an organization as a system, which subsystem encompasses staff development functions?

    A. Support
    B. Operations
    C. Policy
    D. Service

15. A client who has been referred by his physician to a social worker reports that he has come because of "nerves." He says that for the past six months he has been feeling a lot of muscle tension, and is so "keyed up" and "irritable" that he can't concentrate and focus at work. He also has trouble sleeping and can't control his state of worry at home or on the job. According to the DSM-IV, the **MOST** likely diagnosis would be:

    A. Posttraumatic Stress Disorder
    B. Generalized Anxiety Disorder
    C. Dysthymic Disorder
    D. Major Depressive Disorder

16. A social worker observes a parent reaching out to embrace her four-year-old child. When the child approaches, the parent hugs the child, and then with an admonishing tone states, "You should never be so trusting!" In communication theory, this type of interaction observed by the social worker is referred to as:

A. conditional regard
B. double bind
C. emotional blocking
D. cognitive interference

17. A client is seeing a social worker for relationship problems with her boyfriend. She tearfully describes a recent incident in which he was verbally abusive to her. She reports he blames her for his frequent angry outbursts because she does things he considers stupid. Although her friends and family tell her to end the relationship, she says she loves him, but doesn't like the way he treats her. The social worker should **FIRST**:

    A. encourage the client to face the reality of the boyfriend's behavior
    B. explore the client's relationship with family and friends
    C. suggest reading material on abusive relationships
    D. acknowledge the client's ambivalent feelings

18. A woman who recently separated from her husband is seeing a social worker with her children, ages 10 and 16, in family therapy. The initial complaint is that the 10-year-old refuses to attend school. Using a structural family therapy approach, the social worker should **FIRST**:

    A. see the child and mother separately to explore their reactions to the separation
    B. help the mother take charge by encouraging her to insist that the child attend school
    C. arrange for homebound instruction for the child until he returns to school
    D. discuss with the mother her feelings about the recent separation

19. A woman comes to a family agency for help with her marriage. During the first interview with the social worker, she talks rapidly and intensely about her own history of physical illnesses and hospitalizations, her child's problems at school, and her husband's drinking. The **BEST** course of action for the social worker is to:

    A. listen to the client without comment, summarizing at the end of the interview
    B. wait until a pause and ask the client to specify why she came for help
    C. ask the client to elaborate on her husband's drinking and its effect on the family
    D. acknowledge that the client has many troubles and ask which she wants help with

20. In working with reluctant involuntary clients, which of the following areas is the **MOST** important for the social worker to address?

    A. The client's anger at the treatment referral source
    B. The availability of help for the client
    C. The client's ambivalence toward treatment
    D. The social worker's view of the problem for treatment

21. A social work researcher in a mental health clinic wants to measure the effectiveness of group psychotherapy in the social adjustment of recently divorced women. The researcher develops an instrument to measure social adjustment and administers it to 40 divorced women, half of whom are randomly assigned to eight sessions of group psychotherapy. The remaining 20, placed on a waiting list, receive no group psychotherapy. At the end of the eight group sessions the instrument will be re-administered to the 20 group participants and the 20 women on the waiting list. The design being utilized by the researcher is a:

A. static group comparison
B. pretest/posttest control group
C. quasi-experimental
D. one-group pretest/posttest

22. A client has been referred by an Employee Assistance Program (EAP) to a social worker for a maximum of six sessions. The costs for any additional sessions would be the client's responsibility. During the first session, the client describes longstanding personal and relationship problems that she has never resolved, and notes that she is looking forward to finally having the chance to "solve" her problems. Before developing a treatment plan, the social worker should **FIRST**:

    A. support the client's perception that treatment can reduce stress and tension
    B. advocate with the EAP for additional sessions
    C. explore the client's understanding of the referral and the coverage provided
    D. assess the client's capacity and motivation for longterm treatment

23. A cost-benefit analysis in a human service organization is primarily concerned with:

    A. program costs in human and material resources
    B. economic benefits of program goals to the community
    C. the relationship between proposed and actual costs
    D. comparison of alternative means of reaching goals

24. A social worker chairing a task group can **MOST** effectively organize its work by:

    A. rotating the facilitator role among group members
    B. providing relevant written materials to participants prior to the meeting
    C. agreeing to a consensus form of decision-making
    D. specifying the group's objectives

25. In developing a brochure for distribution to prospective clients, a social worker can include all of the following **EXCEPT**:

    A. assurances that treatment will be effective
    B. level of professional credential
    C. highest relevant academic degree
    D. policy on accepting third party payments

KEY (CORRECT ANSWERS)

1. D
2. A
3. A
4. B
5. D
6. D
7. B
8. B
9. D
10. A

11. C
12. B
13. A
14. A
15. B
16. B
17. D
18. B
19. D
20. C

21. B
22. C
23. D
24. D
25. A

EXAMINATION SECTION
TEST 1

DIRECTIONS: Each question or incomplete statement is followed by several suggested answers or completions. Select the one that BEST answers the question or completes the statement. *PRINT THE LETTER OF THE CORRECT ANSWER IN THE SPACE AT THE RIGHT.*

1. A breach of ethical conduct may exist when a social worker: 1.____
   A. discusses sports scores with a client during a session
   B. uses the client's first name
   C. exchanges books to be read for pleasure with a client
   D. exchanges social work sessions for babysitting services by the client

2. A seven-year-old child frequently expresses worry about his parents' whereabouts, is afraid of the dark, cries easily, and complains of frequent stomachaches. The child is MOST likely exhibiting: 2.____
   A. symptoms of abuse and neglect   B. separation anxiety disorder
   C. conduct disorder   D. panic disorder

3. Using behavior therapy for treatment of depression reflects the view that depression is the result of: 3.____
   A. role confusion   B. negative cognition
   C. poor interpersonal skills   D. absence of positive reinforcement

4. A client, referred by his wife, walked into the social worker's office, talking in a loud and threatening manner. He stated that there is no problem except his wife and it is she who should be in therapy. The social worker should FIRST: 4.____
   A. assure the client that he will have the opportunity to discuss his situation
   B. suggest to the client that his behavior indicates that he has a problem
   C. instruct the client to leave the office until he is better composed
   D. ask the client why he believes his wife needs treatment

5. Which of the following characteristics is usually NOT found in families in which incestuous relationships have occurred? 5.____
   A. Enmeshment of family members
   B. Distorted patterns of communication
   C. Symbiotic mother-child relationships
   D. Moralistic attitude toward extramarital affairs

6. Following the resignation of a colleague and the freezing of the colleague's position, social work employees of a non-profit agency confronted the social work administrator. They said they were worried about the financial health of the agency and their job security. In addition they complained about the financial disadvantage they experienced in working for the agency. The administrator agreed to a special meeting designed to address employee issues. When planning how to present budgetary issues in a way that would ensure client care, the administrator should focus on: 6.____

A. acknowledging the legitimacy of employees' concerns
B. explaining the fiscal environment of non-profit organizations
C. charging a committee to develop an alternative budget
D. eliciting input about programs needing priority resource allocation

7. A 28-year-old client with a long-standing history of drug use was referred by a concerned relative to a social worker. In the assessment interview, the client tells the social worker about frequent cocaine use. The social worker should FIRST:

    A. conduct a family interview to gather a comprehensive biopsychosocial history
    B. begin psychotherapy focusing on the reason for drug abuse
    C. refer the client for substance abuse treatment as a prerequisite to individual therapy
    D. evaluate the client's motivation for change

8. A family came to a social worker because of their 11-year-old daughter's behavior in the family. The daughter is an average student and has a group of good friends. Within the family, however, she barely speaks to her parents, refuses to clean her room, and rarely brings her friends home. In describing the daughter's behavior, the parents contradict each other, argue about the severity of the behavior, and disagree on methods of discipline. Using a family therapy approach, the social worker should:

    A. focus on the interpersonal communication within the family
    B. offer the parents the chance to work on the marital relationship
    C. help the daughter to function in the family
    D. involve school personnel with the family to determine the extent of the daughter's behavior

9. A social worker saw an unemployed client whose fee was paid by a concerned family member. As a result of effective treatment, the client resumed employment. Part of the benefit package included HMO coverage for behavioral health care. The client wanted to use this mental health benefit to continue with the social worker, who was already a member of the proper provider panel. To make it possible for the client to use the coverage, the social worker should FIRST:

    A. direct the client to obtain a referral from the primary physician
    B. explain the necessity of formalizing a psychiatric diagnosis
    C. seek pre-authorization for sessions before seeing the client again
    D. inform the client that a case manager controls the number of available sessions

10. A client in her late 20s tells her social worker that she "can't stand" the way she looks, saying that she is overweight and unable to use makeup well, and that she appears sloppy and unkempt, and has little fashion sense. She ends by saying "It's overwhelming to even think about how to change." The social worker should FIRST:

    A. teach the client stress reduction techniques
    B. focus on the clients strengths and skills
    C. establish specific behavioral objectives
    D. work with the client to prioritize her concerns

11. The MOST influential factor in determining the probable success of treatment by a social worker whose client is of a different racial background from that of the social worker is the:

    A. social worker's ability to identify with the client
    B. client's transference toward the social worker
    C. social worker's awareness of self
    D. client's ability to communicate openly with the social worker

12. A couple are being seen jointly for problems "with talking to each other." The husband tells the social worker that his wife was sexually abused as a child and he thinks she still has issues with that. The wife confirms the abuse, but denies that it has any relevance to their marital problems, saying she has dealt with the abuse. The husband continues to focus on this topic even after his wife repeatedly asks him to stop. When she yells at him to "just shut up," he does so and turns away from her. She becomes tense and silent. The social worker's MOST appropriate intervention is to:

    A. suggest that the wife and husband be seen individually
    B. suggest they find a topic on which they have less conflict
    C. recommend that they attend a marriage encounter weekend
    D. process with them the observed communication pattern

13. Which of the following statements is true of BOTH supervision and consultation in social work?

    A. The focus is on a continual process of resolving problems identified by the consultant or supervisor.
    B. The level of responsibility of the consultant and supervisor are the same.
    C. The final decision-making authority rests with the consultant or supervisor.
    D. The consultant or the supervisor focus on helping the social worker deal more effectively with problems or tasks.

14. A social worker asks a young child during an assessment interview, "If I asked your parents what they think about you, what would they say?" The social worker is assessing the child's:

    A. dependence on parents
    B. reality testing
    C. conscience
    D. self-concept

15. The use of silence by a social worker during a session with a client who is expressing a high degree of emotion will be MOST effective in:

    A. demonstrating empathy with the client
    B. relieving the client's tension
    C. developing better rapport with the client
    D. assuring the client that the social worker is listening

16. An adolescent boy in a coeducational inpatient group conducted by a social worker is about to be discharged. The treatment staff recommends that the boy be referred to a group home placement rather than returning home to a chaotic family situation. The group members identify with the boy's feelings of wanting to go home and become furious with the staff for its recommendation. In a group session, they become angry and verbally abuse the social worker. The social worker should FIRST:

    A. explain that the reason the boy should go to the group home is due to the family's instability
    B. explore with the group past negative experiences with group homes
    C. explain to the group that some of the material is confidential because it regards the boy's family and it should not be discussed
    D. acknowledge the group's anger and help members identify the underlying issues

17. Family therapy is contraindicated when:

    A. family members are grossly deceitful and destructive to one another
    B. there is evidence of consistent violation of generational boundaries
    C. family myths and secrets appear to be the family style
    D. the identified client is resistant and unmotivated toward change

18. In establishing a therapeutic relationship with an adult client, the social worker should focus attention on the interpersonal process during:

    A. the initial phase of treatment
    B. the establishment of goals
    C. each phase of treatment
    D. the implementation of goals

19. The major difference between process and outcome evaluation in social work practice is:

    A. outcome evaluation is limited to objective measures; process evaluation involves subjective measures
    B. process evaluation focuses on what was done to achieve results; outcome evaluation is focused on the results
    C. outcome evaluation can be conducted only during the termination stage; process evaluation begins with the assessment stage
    D. data for outcome evaluation is secured from the client; the source for process evaluation data is the social worker

20. During a utilization review phone call, a social worker is asked by the managed care representative to provide specific details of the sexual abuse incidents the client experienced. The social worker should:

    A. provide all requested information to the reviewer
    B. refuse to give specific information to protect the client's privacy
    C. review the release of information with the client prior to providing information
    D. review the managed care contract with the supervisor prior to providing information

21. After careful exploration in psychotherapy regarding mounting anxiety and fear of loss of impulse control, a client decided to seek inpatient admission on a voluntary basis. The social worker arranged for a psychiatric evaluation by a provider approved by the client's managed care insurance company. The psychiatrist refused to support admission and prescribed medication, stating the patient could be stabilized and maintained in the community with appropriate therapy. To help the client understand what happened, the social worker should:

    A. validate the client's plan and send the client for a second opinion
    B. explain the requirements of medical necessity and levels of care
    C. explore the possibility of the client paying for inpatient care
    D. mobilize family members to provide the protection needed by the client

22. In working with adult survivors of childhood sexual abuse, the MOST frequently encountered defense mechanism is:

    A denial
    C. suppression
    B. intellectualization
    D. projection

23. A client is being seen for an initial session by a social worker in private practice. While discussing her history, the client mentions that she has been hospitalized several times for "depression." When the social worker attempts to explore the hospitalizations, the client become tense and guarded, saying it is "old history." She also declares that she won't give permission for those records to be released. The social worker should FIRST:

    A. explore with the client why this topic appears to be upsetting to her
    B. acknowledge the client's right to decide about release of her records
    C. reassure the client that the focus will be on present issues and concerns
    D. assess the client's current level of depression

24. A social worker who tends to be directive and focused on the client's presenting problem is using which of the following therapeutic models?

    A. Object relations
    C. Psychoanalytic
    B. Cognitive behavioral
    D. Existential

25. A hospital social worker is helping a family plan for the home convalescence of a nine-year-old girl injured in an automobile accident. The family reports difficulty with the school district in arranging for a home teacher. When the social worker attempts to contact the administrator responsible for home teacher assignments, the phone calls are not returned. With the child's discharge one week away, the social worker should FIRST:

    A. contact the superintendent of schools about the urgent need for action
    B. request that the primary physician contact the superintendent of schools
    C. send a registered letter to the administrator with the physician's recommendation for a home teacher
    D. arrange follow-up services with the public health nurse who will provide convalescent care

KEY (CORRECT ANSWERS)

1. D
2. B
3. D
4. A
5. C
6. D
7. C
8. A
9. A
10. D

11. C
12. D
13. D
14. D
15. B
16. D
17. A
18. C
19. B
20. C

21. B
22. A
23. B
24. B
25. C

TEST 2

DIRECTIONS: Each question or incomplete statement is followed by several suggested answers or completions. Select the one that BEST answers the question or completes the statement. *PRINT THE LETTER OF THE CORRECT ANSWER IN THE SPACE AT THE RIGHT.*

1. A client whose mother died recently following a long-term illness states to the social worker that he believes that his angry thoughts about his mother caused her death. The client's thoughts are an example of: 1.____

    A. delusions
    B. grandiosity
    C. ideas of reference
    D. magical thinking

2. Parents of a four-year-old child are referred to a social worker after an examination reveals no physical problem preventing the child from being toilet trained. The parents reveal that the child has not been able to separate from them to attend nursery school, and often sleeps with them even though they have tried to get him to sleep in his own room. During the assessment phase, the social worker's MOST important focus is the: 2.____

    A. parents' use of rewards and punishments with the child
    B. early developmental history of each parent
    C. parents' understanding of the child's developmental processes
    D. ways in which the child affects the parents' own relationship

3. A 24-year-old woman tells the social worker that she has felt depressed for the past two to three years. She describes herself as feeling sad, with little energy for work or social activities. She also has difficulty making decisions and concentrating on her work, and has a poor appetite. Assessment information does not reveal an apparent reason for the onset of the depressed mood. The client evidences no delusions or hallucinations. According to DSM-IV criteria, the MOST likely diagnosis for the client is: 3.____

    A. dysthymic disorder
    B. bipolar disorder, depressed
    C. cyclothymic disorder
    D. major depressive episode, recurrent

4. An individual who believes, despite evidence to the contrary, that feelings, thoughts or actions are imposed by an external source, is suffering from: 4.____

    A. delirium
    B. delusion
    C. dissociation
    D. dysphoria

5. Which of the following medications is used primarily for the treatment of psychosis?   5.____

    A. Haloperidol (Haldol)
    B. Alprazolam (Xanax)
    C. Bupropion (Wellbutrin)
    D. Fluoxetine hydrochloride (Prozac)

6. A client manifests the characteristics of the early stages of Alzheimer's Disease. To help the client with the changes in her behavior, the MOST appropriate treatment approach for the social worker to use is to focus on:

   A. an understanding of the client's past behavior to enable her to project her future behavior
   B. providing her family members with a support group of other families with similar problems
   C. treatment sessions structured around whatever the client wishes to discuss
   D. observing the progression of the illness and supporting the client in accepting her losses

7. A new client tearfully reports to the social worker that her father, with whom she is very close, is terminally ill. The client's mother, described by her as "very dependent," has already been calling frequently for support and reassurance. The client says "I just don't know how to cope with dad's illness, my mother's demands and my family's needs," and begins to sob. The social worker should FIRST:

   A. acknowledge the client's feelings of being overwhelmed and sad
   B. discuss a referral for hospice care for the father
   C. identify the client's social and family support network
   D. begin exploring ways the client can set limits for her mother

8. A social worker is seeing a lesbian client who is experiencing feelings of frustration, depression, and sadness related to her inability to conceive a child after unsuccessful treatment for infertility problems. She and her partner are considering adoption, but have been rejected by a local agency because of their same gender relationship. The client feels helpless, and does not think she will be successful in fighting the agency bias against same-gender couples. In assisting the client to formulate goals for intervention, the social worker should:

   A. explore the client's motivation to pursue adoption at this time
   B. evaluate where the client is in her coming-out process
   C. help the client to confront the discriminatory policies of the agency
   D. refer the client for medication evaluation for depression

9. A client is complaining about her friend, stating that she is selfish and insensitive. The social worker asks if this is the same friend whom the client had described the week before as caring and a true friend. The client confirms that it is the same person. The social worker comments that this is a complete change in the client's way of thinking. The social worker is using the intervention of:

   A. Interpretation
   B. Reality testing
   C. Confrontation
   D. Clarification

10. Which of the following actions by a social worker is considered unethical?

    A. Receiving a fee for the referral of a client to another practitioner
    B. Informing the client of fees in advance of services
    C. Engaging in private practice while holding an agency employment
    D. Establishing rates for professional services not commensurate with that of other professionals

11. A social worker, many of whose clients are in crisis, carries a heavy and difficult case load. In discussing the cases with the supervisor, the social worker reports that clients "come in with a laundry list of complaints" and efforts to help them resolve their problems result in the social worker feeling angry and frustrated or distant and bored. The social worker is MOST likely dealing with the issue of:

    A. transference
    B. countertransference
    C. job-related stress
    D. depression

12. When authorization for treatment from a managed care company is requested, the PRIMARY determinant for approval is based upon:

    A. treatment goals that are explicit and measurable
    B. a diagnosis covered by the insurance plan
    C. documentation that medical necessity criteria are met
    D. a treatment plan providing the least restrictive level of care

13. After six marital therapy sessions with a social worker, a couple continued their destructive pattern of fighting. During the next session, the couple began yelling at each other in a loud and threatening manner. The social worker stopped them and stated, "Your situation is hopeless; fight as often as you wish." This technique is known as:

    A. encouragement
    B. reframing
    C. prescribing a ritual
    D. paradoxical directive

14. According to ego psychology, projective identification is a concept that describes the process of:

    A. unconsciously perceiving others' behavior as a reflection of one's own attitudes
    B. consciously imitating the characteristics of a significant other
    C. showing another person how to develop a better self-image through modeling
    D. associating characteristics from a significant person in the past with another in the present

15. The executive director in an expanding nonprofit social service agency increasingly involved the Director of Professional Services (DPS) in overall agency planning and decision-making. To participate and still perform DPS functions, this manager delegated some activities to senior professionals. According to principles of delegation, the DPS could shift:

    A. responsibility for task completion
    B. authority to perform tasks
    C. power and influence
    D. responsibility for managerial decisions

16. In interviewing a client, a social worker seeks concreteness from the client for all of the following purposes EXCEPT to:

    A. avoid emotionally charged topics
    B. elicit the client's specific feelings
    C. clarify a client message
    D. focus on the "here and now"

17. In planning to evaluate social work treatment in an agency, the MOST important consideration is:

    A. the amount of clinical staff time the evaluation will require
    B. whether the results of the evaluation can be applied to other services
    C. information the evaluation will yield for treatment decision-making
    D. involvement of clinical staff in the planning of the evaluation strategy

18. A couple in their mid-50s came to a family agency accompanied by their adult daughter who lives in their home. They describe marital difficulties which began after the husband suffered a mild stroke. The wife said that he has frequent outbursts of anger, has lost interest in his personal care, and is fearful of being left alone. The husband stated that his wife is overprotective of him, and described the daughter as "nervous when I try to do anything for myself." Using a structural family therapy approach, the social worker would focus on:

    A. obtaining a complete history of the marital and family relationships
    B. creating a situation in the interview which would place the husband in a dependent role
    C. exploring with all family members their feelings about the effects of the stroke on family relationships
    D. arranging individual treatment sessions for each family member

19. A social worker used three different techniques with a depressed client, introducing each of the treatment techniques in order over a period of time. To compare the effectiveness of each of the techniques in helping the client reach the treatment goal, which of the following designs should the social worker use?

    A. A-B design
    B. Multiple baseline across behaviors design
    C. A-B-A-B design
    D. Within-series design

20. An adult who has come to a hospital emergency room complains of visual hallucinations, confusion, and restlessness. Physical symptoms include chills, dilated pupils, and nausea. When interviewed by the social worker, the client states, "Nothing is wrong; I just need some sleep. Which of the following substances is MOST likely the cause of the client's condition?

    A. Alcohol
    B. Marijuana
    C. Cocaine
    D. Barbiturates

21. After several sessions in individual treatment with a social worker, a married woman client reveals that she has had an ongoing affair during the last five years. She says that she is unhappy in her marriage but wants to remain with her husband until her children are in college. She believes her husband does not suspect her

infidelity but is often upset that she does not spend enough time with him. The BEST plan for the social worker in this situation is to:

- A. focus the treatment on the client's feelings about the situation
- B. schedule sessions with the entire family
- C. see the couple together
- D. refer the husband to another therapist

22. A social worker has been appointed to the board of directors of a family counseling agency. All of the following are appropriate actions for the social worker as a board member EXCEPT:

- A. determining the performance criteria for the agency director position
- B. reviewing data about utilization of agency services by clients
- C. acting as a paid consultant to agency staff who deliver direct services
- D. serving as chair of a board committee on service delivery

23. For the fifth session with a social worker, a client arrived ten minutes late. Upon entering the social worker's office, the client remained standing and said in an anxious tone, "I know I'm late, but I had other things to do, I just couldn't leave work today." The social worker's BEST response would be to say:

- A. "You seem to think more of your work than you do of coming here."
- B. "Maybe we need to explore what it means to you to come here for our sessions."
- C. "I know that your work is important, but my time is valuable. We will just have less time together today."
- D. "You seem to think that I would be angry with you for being late today. Let's talk about what you anticipated I would say."

24. When reviewing a social worker's performance, the supervisor recognized that the social worker conveyed little empathy toward clients who had recently left welfare and were holding first jobs. In order to help the social worker increase the number of empathetically accurate statements made to clients, the supervisor should:

- A. explain welfare-to-work procedures from the client's perspective
- B. suggest that the social worker enter therapy to become a more empathic person
- C. model empathic communication when engaging with the worker
- D. assert clearly the agency's commitment to supporting these clients

25. Borderline personality disorder is characterized by all of the following characteristics EXCEPT:
- A. intense long-term relationships
- B. primitive delusional fantasies
- C. lack of control of aggressive drives
- D. self-destructive behavior

KEY (CORRECT ANSWERS)

1.	D		11.	B
2.	C		12.	C
3.	A		13.	D
4.	B		14.	A
5.	A		15.	B
6.	D		16.	A
7.	A		17.	C
8.	C		18.	B
9.	C		19.	D
10.	A		20.	C

21. A
22. C
23. D
24. C
25. A

EXAMINATION SECTION
TEST 1

DIRECTION: Each question or incomplete statement is followed by several suggested answers or completions. Select the one the BEST answers the question or completes the statement. *PRINT THE LETTER OF THE CORRECT ANSWER IN THE SPACE AT THE RIGHT.*

1. During an initial interview, a client is observed to speak slowly in a monotone and show little change in facial expression. The client's movements are slow and his posture is stooped. The most likely condition suspected by the worker is

    A. a manic episode
    B. affective disorder
    C. anxiety disorder
    D. depression

    1.____

2. Which of the following is NOT typically included in the "conceptual work" of a human services organization?

    A. Identifying policy options
    B. Drafting policy proposals
    C. Data gathering
    D. Using task forces

    2.____

3. Which of the following procedures is generally performed FIRST in large-group problem-solving?

    A. Dyads are formed.
    B. Group shares an analysis of the problem.
    C. Individuals study papers for 10 minutes.
    D. Quartets are formed.

    3.____

4. After a practitioner has made an assessment of a client's strengths, limitations, and resources, he begins the process of defining problems that will be addressed by specific interventions. Generally, the FIRST step in the process would be to

    A. determine the source(s) of the difficulty in the person-in-environment transaction
    B. describe how the difficulty in the person-in-environment transaction manifests itself
    C. determine the resources in the client and the environment that can be enlisted for change
    D. locate where the difficulty in the person-in-environment transaction manifests itself

    4.____

5. Which of the following is NOT a method involved in the performance-audit method of program outcome evaluation?

    A. Case studies
    B. Process evaluation
    C. Cost finding
    D. Output measurement

    5.____

6. Which of the following is a key accomplishment of Piaget's preoperational stage?

    6.____

A. Conservation
B. The object concept
C. The symbolic function
D. Formal operations

7. A client comes to a social worker to discuss her marital problems. During this first session, the client discloses that she has been abused by her husband for many years and lives in constant fear. The social worker should

A. provide the client with a shelter referral
B. insist that the client not return home
C. report the husband to the police
D. ask the client to bring her husband in for treatment

8. The main problem with using payroll taxes as a funding source for social services or programs is that

A. they have too many prior claimants
B. Social Security and Medicare preempt most shares of employer payrolls
C. they encourage frivolous and unnecessary use of programs and services
D. they are often opposed by special interests

9. Given cultural differences, an untrained social worker from the majority culture in the United States may perceive the relationship between Native American parents' attitudes toward their own children as

A. permissive
B. detached
C. overinvolved
D. severe

10. To begin the social planning process, a team of social workers makes a careful problem assessment. Typically, their NEXT step would be to

A. examine and choose among various courses of action
B. analyze the causes of the problem
C. determine strategy
D. establish goals

11. In order to make clear decisions about the extent of client self-determination, social workers need to understand that a client is truly autonomous only when
   I. there is no coercion on the client from any source to choose one or another option
   II. the person has the opportunity to act on his/her choice
   III. the person has accurate information about the costs and consequences of each option
   IV. there is only one clearly preferable choice available, and the person chooses it

A. I only
B. I, II, and III
C. II and III
D. I, II, III and IV

12. A diagnosis of schizophreniform disorder is consistent with symptoms that have persisted

    A. for more than a day but less than a month
    B. more than a month, but less than 6 months
    C. more than six months, but less than a year
    D. for a period longer than one year

13. A social worker has begun a research project that involves an in-depth study of a multi-generational family. Which of the following terms describes this type of research?

    A. case study
    B. experimental
    C. cross-sectional design
    D. quasi-experimental

14. According to fair employment guidelines, which of the following is an acceptable pre-employment inquiry to put to an applicant?

    A. Whether the applicant is a U.S. citizen
    B. Whether the applicant has ever been arrested
    C. Dates of applicant's attendance or completion of elementary or high school
    D. The language the applicant reads or writes

15. Purposes of the professional social worker/client relationship include
    I. A means for helping the client to unfold his or her story
    II. A source of data for the case
    III. A way to influence client behaviors

    A. I only
    B. I and II
    C. I and III
    D. I, II and III

16. The primary disadvantage associated with the social planning model of community practice is that

    A. planners tend to alienate those members of the bureaucracy that are in the best position to help
    B. there is a tendency for planners to be stuck in a primarily "enabling" role
    C. there is a tendency for the planners to serve the existing power structure
    D. planners are at risk for disciplinary actions by their employers

17. According to DSM-IV, a diagnosis of post-traumatic stress disorder is appropriate if symptoms in general categories persist for at least one month. Which of the following is NOT one of these categories?

    A. Increased arousal
    B. Reexperiencing reactions related to the trauma
    C. Avoidance responses
    D. Disorganized thought or speech

4 (#1)

18. Which of the following statements about the psychoanalytic perspective of social work intervention is TRUE?

   A. Transference is considered the key to discovering the unconscious
   B. Negative, but not positive, transference is a form of resistance
   C. Positive and negative transference are both forms of resistance
   D. transference represents projections of disowned aspects of the self

18.____

19. A family services practitioner meets with a 5-year-old girl who has been removed from the care of her stepfather by the courts because of physical and emotional neglect. She doesn't interact well with other children or adults, doesn't make eye contact with other people, and demonstrates no anxiety when left alone for any period of time. The girl has poor language skills, often repeating herself or using indecipherable grammar. Probably the most accurate DSM-IV diagnosis for this child would be

   A. Reactive attachment disorder of infancy or early childhood
   B. Autistic disorder
   C. Pervasive developmental disorder, not otherwise specified
   D. Communication disorder

19.____

20. "Influencing" skills in client interviewing include each of the following, EXCEPT

   A. Refraining
   B. Directives
   C. Focusing
   D. Feedback

20.____

21. Which of the following is a principle associated with the self-realization approach to social work ethics?

   A. The basis of social life is formed by individual freedom and responsibility.
   B. Human nature is neither essentially bad nor good, but adaptable.
   C. The focus of social work is ideological.
   D. Personal identity is defined by a person's relation to institutions.

21.____

22. A 45-year-old client, a halfway house resident, usually walks the streets of the city during the day, ignoring people but speaking warmly and directly to any pets he meets on his route. The man admits to his social worker that he usually hears the voices of these animals responding in his head. The most appropriate DSM-IV diagnosis for this client is schizophrenia, _____ type.

   A. paranoid
   B. disorganized
   C. residual
   D. undifferentiated

22.____

23. A group leader wants to encourage spontaneity and participation on the part of group members, as well as to bring about a change in members' expectations of other members. Which of the following types of role-playing exercises is most appropriate for this objective?

   A. Role reversal
   B. Doubling

23.____

C. On-the-spot interview
D. Sculpting

24. Which of the following behavior patterns is LEAST likely to be demonstrated by the members of a severely dysfunctional family?

    A. Hypochondriacal obsessions
    B. Extreme overprotectiveness
    C. Chronic complaining
    D. Repressed anger or hostility

25. Which of the following models of social agency policy-making is MOST likely to challenge the status quo?

    A. Technical or analytical
    B. Consensus-building
    C. Entrepreneurial
    D. Value-based

26. The medium of change in the social action model of community practice can best be described as the manipulation of

    A. small task-oriented groups
    B. scarce resources
    C. formal organizations and data
    D. mass organizations and political processes

27. A client complains to a social worker that his marriage troubles stem from his wife's refusal to take on most of the child-rearing and household tasks. After some discussion of the issue, the social worker says, "So you feel you're working as hard as you can and generating most of the family income. But your wife also has a full-time job, and does most of the child-care work-and you also expect her to take care of most of the housework. How does that sound to you?" Here, the social worker is making use of the technique of

    A. paraphrasing
    B. reflection of meaning
    C. confrontation
    D. reflection of feeling

28. The adult family of an 89-year-old woman with dementia related to Alzheimer's disease seeks counseling from a practitioner about how to deal with the changing family situation. As part of his assessment and to help design an intervention strategy, the social worker draws up a family genogram.
    In this context a genogram would be useful for each of the following purposes, EXCEPT

    A. recording the family history of illness
    B. assessing the structure and quality of family relationships
    C. narrowing the context of the illness
    D. identifying sources of support for the client and family members

29. The criteria which generally guide the distribution of scarce resources among people, communities, groups, and organizations include
   I. contribution
   II. equality
   III. compensation
   IV. need

   A. I and III
   B. II and IV
   C. IV only
   D. I, II, III and IV

30. When treating families of patients who are suffering from chronic pain, social work interventions that deal with the issue of _____ are generally most likely to succeed.

   A. the patient's dependence on a spouse or other family member
   B. sexual problems
   C. the adjustment problems of one or more children
   D. the difficulties of the patient's spouse in expressing warmth and acceptance

31. In qualitative evaluations of social work practice, units of analysis typically refer to

   A. clients
   B. types of service
   C. practitioners
   D. points of service delivery

32. In the solution-focused model of social work, which of the following communication skills is generally MOST important for a social worker in working with a client?

   A. Advice
   B. Refraining
   C. Self-disclosure
   D. Feedback

33. A social worker is seeing a couple about their marital problems. Meeting with the social worker was the wife's idea; she says her husband has become increasingly distant and irritable over the past few months. During a recent session, the husband reveals that he's become increasingly anxious about his job. He's a mid-level manager at a large food distributor, and has been passed over for promotion several times in the last few years. He is preoccupied with the small conversations and interactions that have occurred at work, fearing how his co-workers and supervisors will interpret his words and actions. At work he feels restless; at home he has trouble sleeping. When his wife tries to talk to him about work, he refuses. Given these criteria, it's likely that the husband would receive a DSM-IV diagnosis of

   A. generalized anxiety disorder
   B. acute stress disorder
   C. obsessive-compulsive disorder
   D. anxiety disorder not otherwise specified

34. Which of the following would be considered a "mediating unit" in a human service delivery system?

    A. A for-profit service agency
    B. A voluntary service agency
    C. A household unit
    D. A self-help group

35. During an initial interview with a couple who have come to a social worker to deal with the husband's timidity and shyness, the wife agrees to participate in her husband's therapy, stating that she is eager to help. She attends the first two therapy sessions, but afterwards begins to excuse herself, which seems to upset the husband. The MOST appropriate way for the social worker to handle this would be to:

    A. remind the wife that she contracted to participate in her husband's treatment
    B. talk with the wife about the imbalance between her behavior and her expressed promise to help her husband
    C. see the husband for individual therapy since he can benefit from it and work through his feelings about his wife's behavior
    D. approach this as an opportunity to help the husband become assertive, and suggest that he confront his wife about her lack of commitment

36. A person's opinions are a part of his or her individual _____ subsystem.

    A. biophysical
    B. cognitive
    C. affective
    D. behavioral

37. Which of the following is NOT a basic function of a case manager?

    A. Establishing agency objectives and monitoring staff
    B. Remaining aware of all of a client's needs
    C. Monitoring services
    D. Connecting clients to appropriate resources

38. After observing, selecting, gathering, and ordering case data, a practitioner uses inference to make sense of the data. Which of the following is NOT a process of inference?

    A. Making causal connections
    B. Interpreting the interactions among variables in the case
    C. Identifying a client's own capacities and resources
    D. Cross-checking interpretations with the relevant professional knowledge base

39. A social worker is in an interview with a client who was recently convicted of murdering his girlfriend. In order to establish and strengthen the professional relationship with the client, the social worker will need to view the client's crime as

    A. the act of a lost soul in need of redemption
    B. an immoral act that deserves punishment
    C. an uncharacteristic behavior brought on by extreme circumstances
    D. the only thing he could have done, given his subjective circumstances

40. A practitioner views a child's aggressive play as due to a need for power, a wish for revenge, or an attempt to gain attention. The social worker's beliefs are MOST in line with the _____ school of psychotherapy.

    A. psychodynamic
    B. experiential
    C. Adlerian
    D. person-centered

41. During an initial interview, a mother complains that her nine-year-old son refuses to perform basic household responsibilities such as making his bed and picking up his dirty clothes. The son's response is that it's summer and he should be allowed to watch TV or spend time with his friends outside. Applying the Premack principle, a social worker might suggest that

    A. the mother should define clear consequences for not doing assigned chores, and apply those consequences quickly and consistently
    B. the son be permitted to watch television or spend time with his friends only after he has made his bed and picked up his clothes
    C. the son earn points from his mother whenever he does household chores, and that these points be used as credit toward desirable activities such as TV watching
    D. the son be removed from all reinforcers until he complies with his mother's basic requests

42. After several sessions, an unemployed client with low self-confidence, faced with a job interview, has learned to say to herself, "I'll try to do the best I can," instead of her customary thought: "I'll never pull this off." This client's progress is most likely the result of the social worker's use of

    A. cognitive self-instruction
    B. refraining
    C. systematic desensitization
    D. muscle relaxation

43. When a diagnosis for a mental disorder is made and does not completely fit DSM-IV criteria, it should be described as

    A. conditional
    B. latent
    C. provisional
    D. atypical

44. In the psychodynamic model of social work, which of the following communication skills is LEAST likely to be used in a client interview?

    A. Paraphrasing
    B. Open questioning
    C. Summarization
    D. Closed questioning

45. A 45-year-old father maintains exhaustingly high standards of work and achievement for himself, which he passes along to his four children. His insistence on his children's adoption of this attitude has created some family tension. When asked how he came to develop this attitude, the father says it was something his own father (now deceased) never let him forget-that his duty to his family was the most important thing in life, and that it should never be neglected. Which of the following interventions is MOST appropriate for helping the father to explore his feelings about this attitude and its effect on his own family life?

   A. Confrontation and challenge
   B. Building self-esteem
   C. Empty chair
   D. Family sculpting

45.____

46. Which of the following is NOT a trend currently taking place in the traditional American family form?

   A. Single-parent families are more prevalent
   B. Unmarried women are having more children
   C. Remarriage is likely to follow widowhood, rather than divorce
   D. More men and women are living together before being married

46.____

47. A 36-year-old man has been living on the streets for several years. He lives on panhandling proceeds of about $8 a day for food. He is described by neighbors as dirty and irrational, and is often observed warily guarding a collection of colored bits of broken glass. A social worker steps in and has the man taken against his wishes to the closest mental hospital. This is an example of the social work concept of

   A. incompetence
   B. social injustice
   C. divided loyalties
   D. paternalism

47.____

48. Which of the following are necessary consequences of assessing a client as person-in-environment?
   I. Increased case complexity
   II. Social worker's assumption of more numerous and varied roles
   III. Reliance on several different assessment methodologies
   IV. Greater professional "distance" between social worker and client

   A. I and II
   B. II and III
   C. III and IV
   D. I, II, III and IV

48.____

49. Which of the following is NOT an underlying principle of the "functional" casework model?

   A. A The social worker chooses specific interventions to achieve outcomes selected by the client.
   B. Over time, the social worker and client determine how the client will use the services.

49.____

C. The client is the center for change.
D. A social worker engages in a relationship with a client in order to release the client's potential for growth and decision-making.

50. Each of the following factors is believed to increase a client's risk of suicide, EXCEPT

   A. Family history of suicide
   B. Male
   C. Age 22 or younger
   D. Chronic illness

51. A Gulf War veteran has been complaining about the inability to use his left arm. He has seen several physicians, including specialists, and no physical cause for his problem has been found. During an initial interview, the client reveals that during the war he accidentally killed some children with his gun, which he held in his left hand. What is the MOST likely diagnosis?

   A. Malingering
   B. Adjustment disorder
   C. Posttraumatic stress disorder
   D. Conversion disorder

52. The focus of solution-oriented social work can best be described as

   A. observable client behaviors that can be counted and changed
   B. client self-knowledge and ability to make meaning of life
   C. client assets and their utility in resolving problems
   D. making decisions about practical life issues and problems

53. During an initial interview with a married couple, the wife complains to the social worker that the biggest problem in their marriage is the husband's violent temper. The social worker's BEST response to this would be to ask

   A. the husband to explain why he loses control
   B. the wife to explain the problem in greater detail
   C. the husband to confirm or deny this claim
   D. ask the wife what she might be doing to provoke the husband

54. Which of the following is the clearest example of a cognitive minority in the United States?

   A. Jewish Americans
   B. Members of the Libertarian party
   C. People with Down's syndrome
   D. Gays and lesbians

55. A social worker/client relationship characterized by _____ power is considered to be an interface between social work and social justice.

   A. shared
   B. referent
   C. positional
   D. legitimate

56. Within the ecobehavioral model of social work practice, the practice process can be viewed as organic and connected, but with four core functions. The FIRST of these functions is

    A. intervention
    B. envisioning
    C. assessment
    D. engagement

57. Over time, ethnic group names in the United States tend to change (from Negro to black to African-American; from Chicano to Hispanic to Latino). This is a fact that supports the _____ model of ethnicity.

    A. multiculturalism
    B. categorical ethnicity
    C. transactional ethnicity
    D. ethnic competence

58. Based on his research, a social worker may sometimes reach the conclusion that a relationship exists between two variables, when in fact no relationships exists. This is known as a(n)

    A. null hypothesis
    B. negative correlation
    C. type I error
    D. type II error

59. Probably the most important thing a social worker can do to build and strengthen a professional relationship with a client is to

    A. make sure the client understands the worker's background and qualifications
    B. listen in a respectful and nonjudgemental way
    C. avoid subjects that are overly emotional for the client
    D. establish clear, reachable goals

60. DeMause documents a series of historical changes in the authority relations between parents and children in Western cultures. In DeMause's model the current mode of parent-child relations is the _____ mode.

    A. socialization
    B. helping
    C. intrusive
    D. ambivalent

61. A social worker is asked to help rate the ability of a mental health clinic to fund its programs over the next several years. In order to do this, the social worker needs to project income and expenses over the ensuing time period in order to decide which programs to expand or reduce. These forecasting problems are typically solved through the use of

    A. linear programming
    B. PERT charts
    C. difference equations
    D. simulations

62. Research findings indicate that in listing preferences for social worker attributes, individuals from culturally diverse groups are MOST likely to rank

    A. personality similarity as more important than either race/ethnic similarity or attitude similarity
    B. therapist experience as more important than similarity
    C. race/ethnic similarity as more important than attitude similarity
    D. attitude similarity as more important than race/ethnic similarity

63. According to Shaie, people who reach middle adulthood usually develop an understanding of how societal organizations work, and the complex relationships involved. These people are said to have reached the _____ stage of developmental maturity.

    A. responsibility
    B. reintegrative
    C. executive
    D. achieving

64. A social worker begins a session of an intervention group for people who have been arrested for drunk driving by saying: "I know none of you wants to be-here, that you're not interested in what this group has to offer, and that the only reason you're here is because of what will happen to you if you don't show up." After a long pause, one of the group members begins to quietly talk about how the group might be helpful. In this case, the social worker has successfully made use of a

    A. challenge to self-talk
    B. paradoxical intervention
    C. confrontation
    D. reflection of feeling

65. A family services social worker is counseling a couple who are considering divorce. The wife first mentioned divorce because of the husband's serious drinking problem, and has stated her desire to end the marriage if he can't stop drinking. The husband is involved in Alcoholics Anonymous, and has talked in joint sessions about how much it has helped him. Recently, however, the husband has privately revealed to the social worker that he has been lying about attending AA meetings, and that his drinking is worse than ever and begins early in the morning. The husband says he is desperate and needs the social worker to help, and asks the social worker to promise not to tell his wife about the drinking. The BEST possible outcome for this situation would be for the social worker to

    A. disclose the husband's secret to the wife during the next joint session
    B. disclose the husband's secret to the wife privately
    C. give the husband a period of time to disclose the information to his wife, and then withdraw from the case if he refuses to do so
    D. persuade the husband to disclose the information to his wife voluntarily

66. Each of the following is a guideline to be used by a social worker in building a constructive relationship with a client, EXCEPT

    A. View the client as an equal.
    B. Maintain strict confidentiality whenever possible.

C. Use a shared vocabulary of words that are easily understood by the client and that are not offensive.
D. Adopt a completely neutral tone of voice when questioning and responding to the client.

67. Which of the following statements is TRUE about interventions involving insight training?   67.____

    A. Treatment is likely to be relatively short-term.
    B. The goal of treatment is to resolve underlying conflicts or disturbing unconscious processes.
    C. People with emotional or behavioral problems are viewed as clients or consumers of services.
    D. Behavior is viewed as being determined primarily by the environment.

68. Which of the following approaches to intervention is LEAST likely to be successful for an outpatient drug/alcohol counseling program?   68.____

    A. Directive contracting
    B. Behavioral training
    C. Cognitive therapy
    D. Psychoeducation

69. Which of the following political styles should be used to promote an issue that could become controversial if it is perceived to involve major reforms?   69.____

    A. High conflict, polarized
    B. High conflict, consensual
    C. Moderate conflict, compromise-oriented
    D. Low-conflict, technical

70. Which of the following is NOT a guideline that should be used in working with bi- or multi-racial child clients?   70.____

    A. Encourage reflection on the family situation through comments and questions.
    B. Suggest ways in which parents can expose children to their different heritages.
    C. Discourage consideration of physical characteristics.
    D. Help develop a family tree that goes back as far as possible.

71. Advantages associated with group supervision include each of the following, EXCEPT   71.____

    A. Participants learn how to handle many different kinds of cases
    B. Improved management of interpersonal conflict
    C. Increased opportunity for working with advanced staff.
    D. Time- and cost-efficiency.

72. According to Cooper, a person's "connectedness" to others around him or her consists of the dimensions of   72.____

    A. family and community
    B. mutuality and permeability
    C. content and context
    D. permanence and transience

73. A diagnosis of schizophreniform disorder is suitable for clients whose psychotic symptoms are similar to those of schizophrenia and

   A. have existed more than six months
   B. have existed more than one month, but less than six months
   C. have existed more than one year
   D. are related to substance abuse

74. A client comes to a practitioner because her income from a part-time job is not sufficient to support herself and her three children. During her description of the problem, the client begins to talk in an offhand way about her relationship with her mother, whom the client sees as overbearing and critical of the way she is raising her children. After a minute or so of the client's speech about her mother, the practitioner says, "It sounds as if your mother is making things more difficult than they have to be. But let's return for a moment to the subject of your trouble making ends meet." In this instance, the practitioner is making use of an interviewing skill known as

   A. verbal tracking
   B. confrontation
   C. reflection
   D. paraphrasing

75. A hospital social worker is assigned to an eighty-five-year-old cancer patient who the doctors say will most likely die within eight months. The man's doctor, at the request of his children, has not told the man of his prognosis. The client asks the social worker if he is dying. The social worker should tell him

   A. to ask his doctor
   B. to ask his children
   C. the truth
   D. that he is not seriously ill

KEY (CORRECT ANSWERS)

1. D	16. C	31. A	46. C	61. C
2. D	17. D	32. D	47. D	62. D
3. A	18. C	33. A	48. A	63. C
4. D	19. C	34. D	49. A	64. B
5. A	20. C	35. B	50. C	65. D
6. C	21. A	36. B	51. D	66. D
7. A	22. D	37. A	52. C	67. B
8. B	23. A	38. C	53. C	68. B
9. A	24. D	39. D	54. B	69. D
10. B	25. D	40. C	55. A	70. C
11. B	26. C	41. B	56. D	71. B
12. B	27. C	42. A	57. C	72. B
13. A	28. C	43. C	58. C	73. B
14. D	29. D	44. D	59. B	74. A
15. B	30. A	45. C	60. B	75. C

TEST 2

DIRECTIONS: Each question or incomplete statement is followed by several suggested answers or completions. Select the one the BEST answers the question or completes the statement. *PRINT THE LETTER OF THE CORRECT ANSWER IN THE SPACE AT THE RIGHT.*

1. "Axis IV" diagnoses in the DSM-IV include

    A. psychosocial and environmental problems
    B. clinical disorders
    C. personality disorders and mental retardation
    D. global assessments of functioning

    1.____

2. Most of the political opposition to "block grant" funding of social services or programs is based on the perception that

    A. there are too many restrictions and conditions placed on the use of funds
    B. they do not allow for flexibility in program development
    C. they involve complex licensing and classification standards
    D. programs using the funds are often misdirected

    2.____

3. Some members of a therapy group want everyone to be required to provide information about themselves, while others don't want to disclose personal information, but instead prefer to ask questions about other members. Under Yalom's model of group interaction, which of the following approaches should be taken by the social worker?

    A. Explain to all group members that self-disclosure is necessary if group therapy is to work
    B. Interpret the resistance of the members who do not want to self-disclose
    C. Have group members discuss and process the conflict
    D. Have the group members vote on this issue and let the majority decide

    3.____

4. A 12-year-old boy is referred to the school social worker has been referred to the school social worker because of persistent performance problems that have lasted most of the school year. The boy has difficulty organizing tasks and activities, is forgetful and easily distracted, and makes careless mistakes in his school work and other activities. Frequently, the boy does not seem to be listening to the teacher even when he is being directly addressed. Otherwise, the boy has exhibited no other behavior problems. Which of the following DSM-IV diagnoses is consistent with the given conditions?

    A. Attention-Deficit/Hyperactivity Disorder, not otherwise specified
    B. Attention-Deficit/Hyperactivity Disorder, predominantly inattentive type
    C. Oppositional disorder
    D. Conduct disorder

    4.____

5. Which of the following approaches to social work is LEAST likely to focus interventions on the presenting problem?

    A. Client-centered
    B. Solution-focused
    C. Behavioral
    D. Rational/emotive

    5.____

6. Administrators at an agency arrange a meeting of several staff and board members. In a meeting arranged by administrators at a social services agency, several staff and board members are encouraged to express their ideas. It is agreed that for the time being, no one will critique or evaluate these ideas. This type of arrangement is referred to as:

   A. satisficing
   B. the herd mentality
   C. groupthink
   D. the polarization phase

6.____

7. An auditor's opinion about the reliability of data in an agency's financial statements involves a study of both the administrative and internal control systems at the agency. Which of the following is an element of internal control?

   A. Approval
   B. Execution
   C. Authorization
   D. Budget

7.____

8. A social worker assesses a client's communication style during an interview and comes to the conclusion that, in the model of developmental counseling and therapy (DCT), the client's emotional orientation could be described as "sensorimotor." Which of the following questions or statements is MOST likely to enhance the client's emotions?

   A. As you look back on the experience, what type of feelings do you notice?
   B. What are you seeing at this moment as you look back on the experience?
   C. You seem to be upset about this.
   D. How do your emotions change when you take another perspective on this issue?

8.____

9. A recently-widowed man has been to see a practitioner for several sessions after his wife's death. His period of intense grief is over, but he still feels a painful longing for his wife and is experiencing extreme sadness, insomnia, and restlessness. This second stage in the grieving process can generally be expected to peak at a period occurring _____ after the death.

   A. 1 to 3 days
   B. 7-10 days
   C. 2 to 4 weeks
   D. 1 to 3 months

9.____

10. A social worker is treating a single mother and her two children, aged 4 and 6. The mother has just lost her job, and the three of them have moved in with her parents. The mother is depressed and feeling overwhelmed. The BEST structure for treatment in the systemic model would involve

    A. the children first, to assess their primary attachment, and then the mother
    B. the mother and the children
    C. the mother and the grandparents
    D. the mother, her parents, and the children

10.____

11. In single-system studies of social work practice, dependent variables are predicted by means of a(n)

    A. scattergram
    B. baseline
    C. contingency table
    D. celeration line

12. In general, poverty-class families are likely to be characterized in each of the following ways, EXCEPT

    A. isolation from neighbors and relatives
    B. births to unwed parents
    C. high rates of divorce
    D. female-headed, single-parent families

13. In designing a policy proposal, a social services agency first establishes a mission or set of objectives. The NEXT step for the agency is most likely to

    A. devise the content and form of services or benefits
    B. ration scarce resources
    C. design the structure of service or program delivery
    D. orchestrate policy oversight

14. It is a common assumption among social workers that women stay with abusive partners because they fear the consequences of leaving. Research of the issue

    A. refutes the fear with the finding that incidents of abuse decrease substantially following separation
    B. refutes the fear with the finding that women are most likely to say they stay in an abusive relationship because they believe the abusive partner will change
    C. refutes this fear with the finding that women are most likely to say they stay in an abusive relationship because they feel they "deserve the abuse"
    D. confirms this fear with the finding that incidents of abuse increase following separation

15. During a client interview, social worker and client are generally LEAST likely to focus the content of the interview on

    A. contextual factors
    B. the client
    C. family
    D. the main issue or problem

16. According to James Marcia, many adolescents have not yet experienced the kind of crisis that would teach them to explore alternatives or make commitments. These adolescents are described as being in a state of

    A. identity foreclosure
    B. identity moratorium
    C. identity achievement
    D. identity diffusion

17. A 14-year-old girl is referred by the court to family services after being adjudicated guilty of shoplifting. The girl is also not attending school, and her mother is angry with her. The girl is hostile and denies she has any problem, but faced with the choice of incarceration or participating in a program of help with the social worker, she agrees to come in to the family services agency and meet with the social worker. Possible presenting problems (as opposed to presenting "requests") in this case include

    I. shoplifting
    II. family dysfunction
    III. truancy
    IV. peer rejection

    A. I only
    B. I and III
    C. II and IV
    D. I, II, III and IV

18. The client-centered approach to social work is generally NOT recommended for clients who are

    A. formal-operational
    B. focused on a single solution
    C. self-directed
    D. abstract

19. Practitioners who work with immigrant families should keep in mind that regardless of the conditions that existed for them prior to migration, most recently-immigrated individuals and families are likely to

    A. have unrealistic financial expectations of American society
    B. perceive American society as overindulgent
    C. attempt to assimilate too quickly
    D. feel a sense of loss

20. Which of the following is true of a relationship that is described as "authoritative"?

    A. It permits little verbal exchanges.
    B. It involves a close emotional bond between worker and client.
    C. It encourages client independence.
    D. It is associated with a client's social incompetence.

21. Use of the person-in-environment approach to client assessment presents the practitioner with several difficulties. Which of the following is NOT typically one of these?

    A. The possibility that the client may be unable or unwilling to view the case in the same way as the practitioner
    B. The total weight, amount, and complexity of typical case problems
    C. Under-emphasis of the "intractable" problems, such as a terminal illness, that contribute to the problem
    D. Adopting a broad enough perspective to keep track of all relevant case data

22. After setting a general goal to improve housing in an urban neighborhood, a social planning team begins to set specific objectives. Which of the following objectives should probably be considered "essential"?

    I. Rehabilitating 30 housing units in the first year that are structurally sound but not up to code.
    II. Beginning proceedings to condemn and remove all vacant houses that are not judged structurally sound.
    III. Conducting a housing inspection of every house in the neighborhood within the first eight weeks.
    IV. Removing trash from existing "yard" lots and planting trees along five residential streets in the first six weeks.

    A. I and II
    B. II and III
    C. I, II and III
    D. I, II, III and IV

23. Which of the following is NOT a type of intrapersonal intervention?

    A. Cognitive restructuring
    B. Systematic desensitization
    C. Role-playing
    D. Refraining

24. A mother and her eight-year-old daughter report to an initial interview in which the mother describes the child as argumentative, temperamental, hostile, prone to throwing things, and inattentive at school. The mother appears moody and withdrawn. In terms of a diagnosis for the daughter, the social worker would MOST likely suspect:

    A. conduct disorder
    B. bipolar disorder
    C. major depressive disorder
    D. oppositional defiant disorder

25. Which of the following role-playing interventions is probably most useful for providing client practice in self-awareness and self-talk?

    A. Autodrama
    B. On-the spot interview
    C. Mirroring
    D. Role reversal

26. In the social action model of community practice, the social worker's role could most accurately be described as

    A. advocate-negotiator
    B. fact gatherer-analyst
    C. enabler-catalyst
    D. educator-coach

27. Which of the following intervention strategies is LEAST likely to be effective in interventions involving families of Southeast Asian heritage?

A. Limitations on the scope of problems to be addressed
B. A directive rather than collaborative attitude
C. Offering concrete services rather than advice
D. Probing during the work phase

28. The simple fact that clients will be drawn to people who are similar to them is explained by the concept of

    A. consensual validation
    B. formal operations
    C. natural selection
    D. domestic networking

29. A married couple is referred to a practitioner by a school social worker to deal with the excessive truancy of the woman's 15-year-old son from a previous marriage. The stepfather has moved into their house, and a new school year has recently begun. While not an outstanding student, the boy has never had significant behavior problems in school before. The boy's mother was divorced from his father two years ago. When asked, both the boy and his new stepfather say they get along well and enjoy each other's company. The practitioner, guided by inference from these facts, would most likely conclude that the factor that is likely to be having the greatest influence on the boy's truancy is

    A. difficulties in adjusting to a new grade level
    B. his father's withdrawal from the boy's life
    C. the mother's decision to remarry
    D. alcohol or drug use

30. Which of the following statements about the implementation of professional evaluations at a social services agency is generally FALSE?

    A. The supervisor should indicate a willingness to accept evaluation of his own performance from the supervisee.
    B. Evaluation should be a continuous process, rather than an occasional event.
    C. The evaluation should focus on strengths and downplay weaknesses.
    D. The supervisor should discuss the evaluation procedure in advance with the supervisee.

31. Most of the "presenting problems" encountered in social work are related to the _____ subsystems of individual clients.

    A. affective
    B. biophysical
    C. behavioral
    D. cognitive

32. Setting the significance level at .01 (alpha = .01) in social work research means that the chance of

    A. rejecting the null hypothesis when it is false is 1%
    B. rejecting the null hypothesis when it is true is 1%
    C. accepting the null hypothesis when it is false is 1%
    D. accepting the null hypothesis when it is true is 1%

33. Which of the following Is LEAST likely to be a symptom of alcoholic withdrawal?

    A. Transient visual or auditory hallucinations
    B. Decreased heart rate
    C. Grand mal seizures
    D. Nausea or vomiting

34. During an assessment interview, a man who has recently been convicted of child sexual abuse states a belief that he was seduced by the child, and was himself a victim. In this case, the man is making use of

    A. denial
    B. projection
    C. a task-focused coping strategy
    D. an emotion-focused coping strategy

35. Which of the following is generally NOT a guideline to be used by a social worker in building a constructive relationship with a client?

    A. Establish a nonthreatening environment for the client.
    B. In initial contacts, try modestly to "sell" yourself and qualifications.
    C. Tell the client up front about your own moral values and beliefs.
    D. Do not express shock if the client relates troubling details about himself or herself.

36. Evidence in research suggests that AIDS-prevention programs for adolescents are likely to be MOST effective when:

    A. parents openly support the program
    B. educational messages are value-free
    C. peers serve as educators and models
    D. they involve high-profile individuals

37. Most likely, a social worker who attempts to impose judgements on clients will encounter

    A. resistance
    B. legal troubles
    C. further dependence
    D. appreciation

38. Among the words that may be used to begin an open question during a client interview, the word "_____" is most likely to put interviewees on the defensive and create discomfort.

    A. Why
    B. How
    C. Could
    D. If

39. For Bowen, "triangles" form in families in order to:

    A. establish power
    B. restore homeostasis
    C. reduce fusion
    D. establish boundaries

40. A social worker wants to help a recently-widowed client expand her social network. The first step in this process would be to

   A. identify and investigate several dating services
   B. encourage the client to take up a hobby that will facilitate interaction
   C. analyze the client's current social relationships
   D. develop a reward system for network-expanding behaviors

41. In general, social workers who engage in contingency management should make use of
   I. positive reinforcers
   II. negative reinforcers
   III. punishment procedures
   IV. extinction procedures

   A. I and IV
   B. I, II and III
   C. III and IV
   D. I, II, III and IV

42. A social worker continues to work with a 47-year-old client who recently suffered a heart attack after she is discharged from the hospital into her home, which she shares with her husband and two children. The social worker should recognize that the most pronounced concerns during this period are

   A. emotional ties to other family members
   B. relinquishment of the sick role and enhanced productivity
   C. fixations on illness and death.
   D. phobias or inhibitions related to work and sex

43. In the social planning model of community practice, the desired outcome of an intervention is best described as

   A. action for social justice focused on changing policy or policy makers
   B. developed capacity of members to organize and change the impact of local planning and development
   C. local or regional proposals for action by an elected body or human services planning councils
   D. the construction of a multiorganizational power base large enough to influence program direction

44. In deciding whether to use self-disclosure during a client interview, the social worker's most important basis should be

   A. the client's proven ability to make the connection between the social worker's experience and his/her own.
   B. whether or not the self-disclosure will benefit the client
   C. the social worker's ability to self-disclose without getting too emotional
   D. the degree to which the social worker's experience resembles that of the client

45. A client comes to a social worker with multiple problems related to her recent separation from an abusive husband and the economic hardship she and her three children are now suffering. When she sits down with the social worker, the client makes a list of eight specific problems that she would like to change. The MOST appropriate next step during this meeting would be for

   A. the client to examine the list and select the two or three problems of highest priority
   B. the worker to offer a few recommendation, if any, and explain why these problems need to be included on the list
   C. the worker to examine the list and select the two or three problems of highest priority
   D. the client and worker to review and sort the problems into logical groupings

46. Which of the following is a favored skill in consensus-building policy-making efforts?

   A. Process
   B. Mobilization
   C. Political
   D. Analytical

47. Following the social planning model, a team of social workers defines a problem that they believe is in the interest of the community at large. The NEXT step for the team would typically be to

   A. deciding on an arena of action
   B. formulating policy and laying out alternatives
   C. implementing plans
   D. build a network of relationships

48. During an intake interview for determining a client's eligibility for unemployment benefits, the client, a 34-year-old man, tells the social worker he is upset about being unemployed for so long (more than a year), and that he now feels inadequate and unemployable. He doesn't know how he will ever manage to get a job, because most days he just doesn't have the energy to leave his apartment and look for work. These feelings of inadequacy have been with him for several years, though he has never had a major depressive episode. According to DSM-IV criteria, the client is suffering from

   A. depressive disorder not otherwise specified
   B. dysthmic disorder
   C. mood disorder not otherwise specified
   D. cyclothymic disorder

49. During an initial interview, members of a family present the oldest teen-age daughter as the problem. The girl is constantly in trouble at school and is defiant at home, especially with her mother. The girl's father is extremely moralistic, with high behavioral expectations for his daughter. The father does reveal, however, that as a teenager he was often in trouble with the law, and spent some time in juvenile detention. A practitioner working from the object relations perspective would suspect that the girl's symptoms are an expression of

   A. parental superego lacunae
   B. acting out

C. splitting
D. projected identification

50. At a general services agency, a social worker witnesses a homeless woman's being denied service because she can't provide proof of residence or source of income. The social worker should

    A. ignore the encounter as a colleague's professional decision
    B. confront the interviewer and insist that the woman be seen, since her needs are more important than administrative red tape
    C. ask the woman into his/her office and offer to advocate on her behalf to the agency
    D. ask the woman into his/her office and refer her to an agency that doesn't have residency or income requirements

50.____

51. A social worker begins treatment planning for the severely dysfunctional family of an 8-year-old child with physical and developmental disabilities. In formulating a treatment plan, the social worker should keep in mind that most severely dysfunctional families tend to

    A. project multiple "doomsday" scenarios in the distant future
    B. focus on present-day difficulties at the expense of long-range planning
    C. dwell on past problems and perceived injustices
    D. voice their grievances to people outside the family

51.____

52. A social planner in a low-income community wants to plan programs that will deal with the problem of high unemployment. The planner needs to know not only how many unemployed people are in the community now, but also how many people will be unemployed at any particular time in the future, and how those numbers will vary given certain conditions. Probably the best way to trace employment rates over time and within differing conditions is through the use of

    A. the critical path method
    B. linear programming
    C. difference equations
    D. the Markov model

52.____

53. A social worker receives a subpoena for portions of a client's case record. The subpoena was requested by a divorce lawyer who represents the client's ex-spouse. Which of the following is TRUE?

    A. If the client hasn't given the social worker permission to disclose the requested information, the social worker should do his/her best to convince the court that the information should not be disclosed.
    B. The social worker should disclose the information only if the sole alternative is to spend time in jail for contempt of court.
    C. The social worker should balance the threat to his client's privacy by filing a subpoena requesting private information about the ex-spouse.
    D. If the social worker is faced with incarceration or a fine, he/she should work to convince the client that disclosure is warranted.

53.____

54. In competence-oriented social work practice, assessment is understood as a process of identifying and understanding

54.____

A. environmental factors that are blocking the client's ability to resolve the presenting problem
B. the psychological subtext that causes a person to relate to his or her environment in a particular way
C. the existing social network that can be called upon to help the client achieve necessary changes
D. the person's capacity to deal with environmental challenges at any one time

55. A practitioner arrives at the workplace on morning to find a neatly-wrapped package waiting for her. The package contains an expensive crystal vase from the parents of a 17-year-old current client, with a card thanking the practitioner for all her hard work. The practitioner should:

    A. refuse the gift
    B. accept the gift and thank the parents graciously
    C. return the vase to the store where it was purchased and not mention it to the parents
    D. donate the vase to a charitable organization

56. During an interview with a young single mother, the practitioner records several statements that indicate a lack of self-esteem, along with self-defeating thoughts. Though the client doesn't acknowledge her behaviors as such, her behaviors refusing to report to a job interview because she knows she is underqualified, for example appear to be self-defeating. Which of the following models of social work would be most useful in formulating an intervention for this client?

    A. Task-centered
    B. Behavioral
    C. Psychodynamic
    D. Cognitive-behavioral

57. A social worker suspects that a client is manic, and asks if the client has ever felt unusually excited or energetic. The client answers yes. The social worker then proceeds to ask several screening questions. Which of the following questions would be LEAST helpful in providing evidence of mania?

    A. During that time, did you ever do things that could have hurt or injured you?
    B. Did you feel tired or run down at the end of the day?
    C. Did you feel easily distracted or drawn to unimportant details?
    D. Did you lose a job or a friend during the time you felt unusually energetic?

58. Which of the following statements about suicide is generally FALSE?

    A. Most suicidal individuals can be considered to be relatively rational.
    B. Most people who attempt suicide are ambivalent about their desire to die.
    C. Most people who commit suicide do so when they are severely depressed.
    D. Suicide attempts are commonly preceded by a communication of the intent to commit suicide.

59. A social services agency plans to install a computerized information system that will maintain client records and help with budgeting and scheduling tasks. The most efficient approach to budgeting for a technology project involves allocating funds among each of the following categories, EXCEPT

A. hardware
B. data migration
C. software
D. support personnel

60. A client who has suffered sexual abuse, if he or she progresses through the recovery process in typical fashion, will usually begin with a response characterized by

    A. rage
    B. guilt
    C. denial
    D. catharsis

61. Which of the following models of social agency policy-making generally involves the highest degree of conflict?

    A. Value-based
    B. Consensus-building
    C. Technical or analytical
    D. Entrepreneurial

62. The mission of the social work profession is rooted in a set of core values. Which of the following is NOT generally considered to be one of them?

    A. Service
    B. Egalitarianism
    C. Dignity and self-worth
    D. Competence

63. A 30-year-old client, recently diagnosed as HIV-positive, is currently living with his brother and sister-in-law because he recently lost his job and was then evicted from his apartment Although his family is aware he is gay, they don't know that he is HIV-positive. The client tells the social worker he has avoided telling his family because he is afraid of their reaction. The social worker should

    A. ask the client to explain his fears about telling his family
    B. ask the client to bring his brother into the next session
    C. address the underlying issues of the client's lack of responsibility in his personal and professional life
    D. refer the client to a support group for unemployed individuals with AIDS

64. A social worker wants to evaluate a relief program for Hmong women taking care of elderly relatives in a community. The program has suffered from lax participation, given the number of Hmong people in the community. A social worker wants to speak with the women in the community who did not respond to the outreach initiative, and begins by visiting with some caregivers who are known to the program. After gaining the trust of these women, the social worker asks for the names of women they know who are in a similar situation. The social worker's approach in this case is

    A. maximum variation sampling
    B. snowball sampling
    C. convenience sampling
    D. typical case sampling

65. A social worker who decides on a case-by-case basis whether to intervene in a client's life is most likely using the value system of _____ as an ethical guide.

    A. distributive justice
    B. communitarianism
    C. clinical pragmatism
    D. situational ethics

66. The FIRST phase of an intervention in the rational self-analysis model involves a statement of

    A. behavioral goals
    B. emotional goals
    C. self-talk
    D. facts and events

67. Most social services with families takes on the _____ unction of the family as the point of departure for intervention.

    A. consumptive
    B. biophysical
    C. affective
    D. productives

68. A supervisor tells a social worker that she wants to observe a supervisee's client interview through a one-way mirror. The worker agrees. The supervisor should advise the worker that he

    A. must obtain informed client consent only if the session is to be recorded or videotaped
    B. must obtain client consent on both the observation and its use
    C. does not need to obtain client consent since the purpose of the observation is supervision
    D. does not need to obtain client consent, since consent was implied with the signing of a release form during the intake interview

69. According to Finestone, the factors in a client's case that maintain his/her difficulty but are also amenable to change are defined as

    A. causal factors
    B. effective determinants
    C. non-point sources
    D. dependent variables

70. A social worker's program evaluation shows clearly that as the implementation of a parenting-skills course moves into urban neighborhoods, incidents of reported child abuse and neglect decline. The relationship between the classes and the prevalence of abuse and neglect can be described as

    A. perfect correlation
    B. positive correlation
    C. normal distribution
    D. negative correlation

71. Which of the following statements about a DSM-IV diagnosis is TRUE?

    A. By itself, it is a sufficient basis for developing a treatment plan.
    B. It is an early or intermediate step in the treatment planning process.
    C. It usually marks the end of the treatment planning process.
    D. It should be made with DRG status in mind.

72. Which of the following behaviors is LEAST likely to be considered unethical by social work professionals?

    A. Accepting a client's invitation to a special occasion
    B. Inviting a client to a party or social event
    C. Becoming friends with a client after termination
    D. Buying goods or services from a client

73. Many feminists believe that there is no difference in the nature of men and women, and that inequality is a problem only when it is excessive or results from discrimination. These feminists are described as

    A. liberal
    B. reactionary
    C. radical
    D. socialist

74. A member of a group that was formed to teach parenting skills approaches a social worker and reveals that she's experiencing a great amount of stress in caring for her elderly mother. After a discussion of the woman's situation, the social worker suggests that the woman contact a local home health care agency, and gives her the phone number of a specific contact person at the agency. In this situation, the social worker is performing the role of

    A. advocate
    B. mediator
    C. enabler
    D. broker

75. Management staff at a social services agency come together to view a record of the agency's assets, liabilities, and net assets. The staff are looking at a(n)

    A. inventory
    B. operating statement
    C. revenue-expense analysis
    D. balance sheet

KEY (CORRECT ANSWERS)

1. A	16. D	31. C	46. A	61. A
2. D	17. C	32. B	47. D	62. B
3. C	18. B	33. B	48. B	63. A
4. B	19. D	34. B	49. D	64. B
5. A	20. C	35. C	50. D	65. D
6. A	21. C	36. C	51. A	66. D
7. D	22. C	37. A	52. D	67. C
8. B	23. C	38. A	53. A	68. B
9. C	24. D	39. B	54. D	69. B
10. D	25. B	40. C	55. A	70. D
11. D	26. A	41. A	56. D	71. B
12. A	27. D	42. D	57. B	72. A
13. C	28. A	43. C	58. C	73. A
14. D	29. C	44. B	59. B	74. D
15. A	30. C	45. B	60. C	75. D

EXAMINATION SECTION
TEST 1

DIRECTIONS: Each question or incomplete statement is followed by several suggested answers or completions. Select the one the BEST answers the question or completes the statement. *PRINT THE LETTER OF THE CORRECT ANSWER IN THE SPACE AT THE RIGHT.*

1. At the outset of treatment, a client tells the social worker that she must promise never to involuntarily hospitalize her, no matter how depressed or suicidal she may seem. In formulating a response to this request, the social worker should use the underlying ethical principle of

    A. the need to do whatever is necessary to maintain a therapeutic relationship with a client
    B. never making a promise that is in conflict with legal and ethical requirements
    C. the client"s right to self-determination
    D. the understanding that the client has legitimate, defensible reasons for making this request

1.____

2. For a Gestalt therapist, a primary goal of treatment is to help the client

    A. integrate the present with his/her past and future
    B. develop a "success identity"
    C. integrate the functioning of his/her mind and body
    D. incorporate the external into the internal

2.____

3. What is the term for a social system that is part of a larger system and made up of several smaller systems?

    A. Focal system
    B. Schema
    C. Holon
    D. Gemeinschaft

3.____

4. The most commonly occurring psychological disorders are _____ disorders.

    A. Dissociative
    B. Psychosexual
    C. Mood
    D. Somatoform

4.____

5. In the early stages of problem-solving communication training with a family, the practitioner should FIRST assess

    A. family cognitions about communication/arguments
    B. the history of the problem
    C. family assets
    D. specific skill deficits

5.____

6. An intern at an agency for the chronically mentally ill meets with a 24-year-old client who has been referred by his family doctor. The primary basis for this referral is the client's isolation from peers and general lack of social skills. In many ways, the client reminds the intern of the quiet, studious friends she made in graduate school, who had very little time to socialize because of studies and part-time jobs. The client tells the intern he doesn't think he belongs in this place, and she silently agrees, though her supervisor and more experienced workers seem to believe that this is the right place for him. In her assessment of this client's situation, the intern has relied on the _____ heuristic.

   A. theoretical
   B. schematic
   C. availability
   D. representativeness

7. Which of the following types of feminism proposes that men and women have different values due to the structure of sex and gender roles in society?

   A. socialist
   B. reactionary
   C. radical
   D. liberal

8. The most significant problem with establishing "comparable worth" at an agency is that

   A. males and females may use different strategies to reach the same decision or solution
   B. the job evaluation techniques themselves may be gender-biased
   C. job evaluation techniques are not as useful for very complex jobs
   D. it is difficult to compare achievement across different domains

9. A social worker decides that solution-focused therapy is the most appropriate approach for a family that has come to see her about financial problems. The social worker's FIRST intervention would be to

   A. discuss time constraints and make sure the family knows the intervention will be brief
   B. get a clear picture of how the system functions
   C. get a history of the origins of the symptoms
   D. discuss how things would be for the family if the problem was already solved

10. Social service agencies, in attempting to make a certain program more efficient and useful, may sometimes get lost in pursuing a prescribed means of service delivery at the expense of accomplishing program goals. This is known as

    A. output loss
    B. goal displacement
    C. bounded rationality
    D. organizational shaping

11. According to Elkind, the most significant descriptor of adolescent thought is

    A. concrete
    B. irrational

C. egocentric
D. moralistic

12. In a program evaluation, which type of data is concerned primarily with whether or not the program goals are being met?

    A. throughput
    B. process
    C. product
    D. input

13. Which of the following problems or disorders is LEAST likely to be changed through psychotherapy?

    A. Anorexia nervosa
    B. Conduct disorder
    C. Antisocial personality disorder
    D. Compulsive behavior

14. The record-keeping requirements at a typical social services agency require the completion of a review treatment plan at an interval no longer than

    A. after every client contact
    B. weekly
    C. every 30 days
    D. every 90 days

15. For social workers, it is usually most appropriate to view a woman's separation from an abusive husband as

    A. a series of losses which initiates a mourning process
    B. a solution that must be accomplished as quickly as possible
    C. a partial process at best if children are involved
    D. the best of all possible solutions to the problem of domestic abuse

16. Formative policy research at social services agencies

    A. is usually conducted in response to legislative mandates
    B. focuses on policy development rather than on its impact on clients and agencies
    C. identifies social policy as the independent variable
    D. is based entirely on output goals

17. Abusive families are most often characterized by

    A. openness and affection
    B. rigid boundaries and clear roles
    C. a strong parental subsystem
    D. denial and enmeshed boundaries

18. The principal assessment tool for clinicians working from the intergenerational perspective on the family is the

    A. life cycle matrix
    B. social history

C. genogram
D. ecomap

19. The "output goals" of a social service program are MOST likely to include

    A. specified ratings of services by clients on a standardized scale
    B. observable effects on a given community or clientele
    C. the number of units of service provided
    D. the number of clients served

20. A 35-year-old client, a high school teacher, reports to a practitioner at an outpatient clinic and reports the following incident: he, a high school teacher, was in the middle of a lesson during a class period that had been particularly difficult for him over the past several months, because the class was large and often noisy. During the middle of today's lesson, the client suddenly began to sweat profusely and his heart started to race. He continued with the lesson but soon felt dizzy and fearful that he was about to die. The feeling was so overwhelming that he had to leave the class unattended and retreat to the teacher's lounge, where he was found sitting alone and trembling. The client's physician has found no evidence of medical problems. The most likely DSM-IV diagnosis for this client would be

    A. panic disorder
    B. posttraumatic stress disorder
    C. dissociative disorder
    D. social phobia

21. Which of the following statements reveals a client with a formal-operational emotional orientation?

    A. I'm so sad right now that my stomach hurts. I haven't eaten all day.
    B. I suppose there are two different ways of looking at this. On one hand, these arguments are really painful, but I know I have to set limits for my son and it's part of my role as a parent. I know he needs to find his own space, but his decisions are sometimes questionable.
    C. I feel great about the new relationship I'm in. I think I've met the perfect man.
    D. As I think about it, I feel bad because it seems as if we've been arguing a lot lately. It's almost a ritual--every time I get ready to leave the house, an argument starts.

22. The purpose of the mental status examination in psychotherapy is

    A. personality testing
    B. to make a diagnosis
    C. reality testing
    D. to determine the severity of psychotic symptoms

23. Which of the following interviewing skills is most useful for discovering the deeply held thoughts and feelings underlying the client's experience?

    A. Confrontation
    B. Open-ended questioning
    C. Focusing
    D. Reflection of meaning

24. A client who has a history of hypomanic and major depressive episodes would have a diagnosis of   24.____

    A. Hypomanic disorder
    B. Cyclothymic disorder
    C. Bipolar I disorder
    D. Bipolar II disorder

25. Which of the following theoretical frameworks establishes equity and distributive justice as its ideal ends of development   25.____

    A. Behavioral/social exchange
    B. Ego psychology
    C. Symbolic interactionism
    D. Structural functionalism

26. A "Theory X" manager in an organization is likely to   26.____

    A. adopt a team approach to problem-solving
    B. use tangible rewards and sanctions to shape employee behavior
    C. work to set up and maintain a work environment that promotes growth and creativity
    D. assume that subordinates want to work toward organization goal attainment

27. Which of the following is generally NOT recommended as part of an intervention with a Native American client who follows older traditions?   27.____

    A. Serving food
    B. Emphasizing the past
    C. Giving gifts
    D. Including friends and family

28. The process of transforming a piece of legislation into a specific program or policy, by means of identifying specific guidelines and operating procedures to be used in administering the program, is known as   28.____

    A. rationalization
    B. promulgation
    C. consignment
    D. confederation

29. Which of the following is NOT an ego-defense mechanism?   29.____

    A. Regression
    B. Reality testing
    C. Displacement
    D. Sublimation

30. Which of the following is probably the MOST appropriate candidate for an intensive, heterogeneous outpatient therapy group?   30.____

    A. A paranoid person
    B. A person with bipolar II disorder

C. An alcoholic or drug addict
D. A person with brain damage

31. In removing intracultural barriers to achievement for clients of color, interventions should be aimed at

    A. active encouragement of family involvement
    B. recognition and affirmation of client system strengths
    C. changes in institutional policies, practices, and administration
    D. improved educational/vocational opportunities through greater teacher/employer awareness of diversity, history and customs

32. Which of the following is a means-tested program?

    A. Medicare
    B. Social Security
    C. Public education
    D. Police protection

33. One of the greatest risks associated with too little self-disclosure in the group therapy process is

    A. severely limited reality testing
    B. low group cohesiveness
    C. yielding an inappropriate amount of member control
    D. severe dependence

34. In behavioral therapy, the systematic desensitization process, usually performed by dis-associating a neutral stimulus from a situation that has created fear or anxiety, is also known as

    A. extinction
    B. aversion therapy
    C. overcorrection
    D. counterconditioning

35. The primary function of reflecting feelings during a client interview is to

    A. help the client sort out mixed or ambivalent feelings
    B. grounding the worker and client in concrete experience
    C. bring out additional details of the client's emotional world
    D. make implicit, sometimes hidden emotions clear to the client

36. Which of the following is NOT a privileged relationship during the prosecution of child abuse?

    A. Priest-confessor
    B. Lawyer-client
    C. Psychotherapist-patient
    D. Physician-patient

37. According to ego psychology, the ego

A. mediates between erotic energies and superego constraints
B. is a drive for pleasure
C. imposes a set of rules to control unbridled pleasure-seeking
D. offers ideals for the individual to strive for

38. Which of the following statements reveals a discrepancy that is external to the speaker? 38.____

    A. I don't mind talking about that at all.
    B. I wanted to go to business school, but my grades weren't good enough.
    C. My mother is a saint, but she doesn't respect me.
    D. This is a nice office. It's too bad it's in this neighborhood.

39. During an intake interview for a woman who has committed a violent crime, the clinician notes that whenever the woman talks of the act she does so without any emotion—anger, shame, guilt, or sadness—whatsoever. From the psychoanalytic perspective, the woman is using the defense mechanism of 39.____

    A. isolation
    B. fantasy formation
    C. repression
    D. rationalization

40. A humanist, looking at an individual's misbehavior, would conclude that a person who acts badly is 40.____

    A. suffering from a kind of illness
    B. experiencing a detachment from her moral compass
    C. willfully disregarding the norms which characterize her community
    D. reacting to the deprivation of her basic needs

41. Clinicians in private practice are generally paid for 41.____
    I. direct services to clients
    II. number of hours on the job
    III. indirect services

    A. I only
    B. I and II
    C. II only
    D. I, II and III

42. A clinician is meeting with a transactional group for the first time and works intensely at studying the members and their transactions. In the early stages of work with this group, the clinician's greatest challenge is likely to be 42.____

    A. defusing conflict between members
    B. identifying the self-talk or cognitions that lie behind a transaction
    C. heading off the tendency toward subgroupings
    D. determining which ego state a transaction comes from

43. A social worker has been seeing a client for several months and has developed a good working relationship. The client loses her job and cannot afford to pay for therapy. Under the social worker's professional code and value system, the BEST option in this case would be to 43.____

A. refer the client to low-cost therapy from another provider
B. allow the client to divert payments until she gets another job
C. provide the therapy free of charge until the client can find employment
D. reduce the fee for this client and/or offer her shorter sessions

44. "Acceptance" in the therapeutic relationship mean that the practitioner

   I. separates the client from her behavior
   II. indicates approval of the client's behavior
   III. expresses sympathy for the client
   IV. demonstrates tolerance for client's behavior

   A. I only
   B. I and II
   C. II, III and IV
   D. I, II, III and IV

45. According to Papernow, most people first enter a stepfamily with

   A. a clear awareness of the reality of their situation
   B. a growing sense of realistic intimacy with new family members
   C. the fantasy that they will rescue the new partner and any children from the deficiencies of a previous marriage
   D. a feeling of resentment toward new family members who place new demands on their time, money, and other resources

46. An ideal therapeutic relationship in social work is one that

   A. connects the client with the proper support services
   B. allows and helps the client's capacity to work out his own issues
   C. is an ongoing source of support
   D. the client can rely upon as a problem-solving tool

47. Which of the following is NOT characteristic of a clinician who is conducting reality therapy with a client?

   A. Viewing mental illness labels as destructive
   B. Focusing on behavior rather than feelings
   C. Discouraging value judgements
   D. Not offering sympathy

48. In general, a DSM-IV diagnosis of a specific disorder includes a criterion of

   A. no medical involvement
   B. a clinically significant impairment or distress in a social or occupational area
   C. an identifiable etiology
   D. distress that has exceeded a period of 8 weeks

49. A client interview is interrupted by a long silence that makes the social worker uncomfortable. The FIRST thing the social worker should do is

   A. inform the client that of his/her (the worker's) discomfort and observe the client's reaction
   B. restate the last words spoken by the client

C. say, "I wonder why you're so quiet"
D. study the client to see if he/she appears comfortable with the silence

50. A social worker is seeing a Latino family that immigrated to the United States several years ago. The social worker is not Latino. The family often arrive late for their sessions, causing some scheduling problems—and mild annoyance—for the social worker. The best way for the social worker to handle this would be to

    A. be aware that time may be perceived differently in their culture and invite them to discuss what being late means to them
    B. understand that being late is probably an expression of cultural resistance to disclosing family issues
    C. be aware that time may be perceived differently in their culture, and take a more flexible approach to beginning scheduled sessions
    D. consider referring the family to a Hispanic therapist

51. The foundation of clinical supervisory techniques—and the focus of supervision—is/are typically

    A. case material
    B. educational assessment
    C. long-term practitioner development goals
    D. practitioner attitudes and values

52. A practitioner grew up as the oldest child of alcoholic parents, and was often placed in the role of parent to his three younger siblings. In order to establish solid therapeutic relationships with his clients, the most important challenge this practitioner will probably face is

    A. being able to trust that clients have the capacity to work through their problems
    B. being able to see clearly the problems faced by alcoholic clients
    C. the risk that he will impose an undue level of responsibility on clients early in the intervention process
    D. a lack of faith in his ability to help clients change

53. A married couple and their two teenage sons see a clinician for the first time for help with what they view as an unhealthy spirit of competition between the two boys. The clinician observes the family's interactions and characterizes them as high-functioning and relatively flexible. Which of the following models of intervention is probably MOST appropriate for this family?

    A. Structural-functional
    B. Strategic
    C. Experiential
    D. Solution-focused

54. According to the lifespan perspective of human development and behavior, development is NOT

    A. contextual
    B. historically embedded
    C. unidirectional
    D. lifelong

55. The sole motivation for a client's feigning illness in factitious disorder is to

   A. obtain prescription drugs
   B. draw attention away from his/her psychological problems
   C. assume a sick role.
   D. escape material and everyday responsibilities

56. In school, an 8-year-old boy has considerably impaired social interactions with other children, along with severely impaired language skills. The boy also pulls at his hair constantly, sometimes leaving ragged bald patches, and often bites himself, leaving wounds and scars that his parents have made the primary concern for treatment. Appropriate diagnoses for this boy include
   I. Asperger's disorder
   II. Stereotypic movement disorder
   III. Autism
   IV. Mental retardation

   A. I and II
   B. II and III
   C. III only
   D. IV only

57. In order to ensure a margin of error no greater than 5%, what is the size of the sample required to represent a population of 10,000?

   A. 108
   B. 370
   C. 1235
   D. 9,500

58. Social learning theory recognizes each of the following as a key factor in human development, EXCEPT

   A. cognition
   B. heredity
   C. behavior
   D. environment

59. According to Annon, clients in sex therapy need interventions at very specific levels. The first of these levels is

   A. specific suggestions
   B. intensive therapy
   C. limited information
   D. permission

60. Which of the following is named as the etiological agent for adjustment disorder?

   A. Depressed mood
   B. Stress
   C. Sudden trauma
   D. Organic chemistry imbalance

61. Social workers generally observe several distinct characteristics in the life cycle of poor African-American families. Which of the following is NOT one of these?

    A. Households that are frequently female-headed and isolated from the community
    B. A scarceness of resources that compels a reliance on government institutions
    C. A truncated life cycle with less time to resolve developmental tasks
    D. A life cycle punctuated by numerous unpredictable life events

62. A 50-year-old client has been significantly depressed for more than a year. For the past two months, the client has been convinced that he has developed lung cancer. The most appropriate DSM-IV diagnosis for the client would be

    A. conversion disorder
    B. major depressive episode
    C. somatoform disorder, not otherwise specified
    D. hypochondriasis

63. Persuasive arguments for flexible-rate fee schedules include
    I. Services more accessible to disadvantaged clients
    II. Endorsements of insurers and other third-party organizations
    III. No means testing
    IV. Consistency with consumer protection laws

    A. I only
    B. I and III
    C. I, II and IV
    D. I, II, III and IV

64. The psychoanalytical perspective views _____ as the most powerful and pervasive defense mechanism.

    A. projection
    B. rationalization
    C. repression
    D. denial

65. Which of the following approaches to client interviewing is MOST likely to make use of interpretation or reframing?

    A. Psychodynamic
    B. Solution-focused
    C. Client-centered
    D. Behavioral

66. When a clinician is on a provider panel for a managed health care company, he or she:

    A. is guaranteed a certain number of referrals from this company per year.
    B. has met the qualifications for company, and has no guarantee of referrals.
    C. agree to see any referral within your specialty.
    D. will receive a full fee from the company when he/she sees a client

67. When a therapeutic relationship is functioning on the cognitive level, the therapist will probably engage in each of the following processes, EXCEPT

A. highlighting inconsistencies
B. reassuring
C. refraining
D. asking key questions

68. Several days after losing her job, a woman becomes so depressed that she is unable to get out of bed until well into the afternoon, and rarely leaves her home. By the time she reports to a practitioner for treatment, she has been depressed and had trouble sleeping for about 4 months. The most appropriate DSM-IV diagnosis for this client is

    A. major depressive episode
    B. dysthmic disorder
    C. adjustment disorder with depressed mood
    D. depressive disorder, not otherwise specified

69. The NASW code's prohibition of dual relationships is most likely to be challenged by social workers who

    A. are part of an interdisciplinary team
    B. live and work in rural areas
    C. are involved in direct practice
    D. perform supervisory functions

70. Many practitioners make use of informal assessment instruments such as self-reporting questionnaires, indexes, and profiles. The main risk associated with these instruments as assessment tools is that they

    A. often put the client on the defensive
    B. may place too much emphasis on relatively unimportant details
    C. suggest that the practitioner may be lazy or incompetent
    D. often provoke client dissembling

71. The term "active listening" mostly refers to a person's ability to

    A. indicate with numerous physical cues that he/she is listening
    B. take an active role in determining which information is provided by the client
    C. concentrate on what is being said
    D. both listen to the client and accomplish other meaningful tasks at the same time

72. Which of the following is a latent function of the family unit?

    A. Economic production
    B. Socialization of children
    C. Provision of emotional support to members
    D. Contribution to institutional arrangements

73. Current knowledge of post-traumatic stress disorder (PTSD) indicates that if the initial stage of anxiety and obsession with the trauma persist for longer than _____, the patient then enters stage 2, or acute PTSD.

    A. 5-10 days
    B. 4-6 weeks
    C. 8-12 weeks
    D. 3-6 months

74. After making contact with a person in crisis and establishing a relationship, a clinician faces the task of examining the dimensions of the problem, in order to define it. Which of the following is NOT typically a task of this phase of crisis intervention?

    A. Exploring alternatives
    B. Assessing the dangerousness or lethality of the situation
    C. Identifying the precipitating event that led to the crisis
    D. Detailing a client's previous coping methods

75. In general, administrative evaluation at a social services agency differs from practice evaluation in that administrative evaluation is

    A. external to the supervisory relationship
    B. continuous
    C. basically self-contained
    D. specific

KEY (CORRECT ANSWERS)

1. B	16. B	31. A	46. B	61. A
2. C	17. D	32. A	47. C	62. B
3. C	18. C	33. A	48. B	63. A
4. C	19. C	34. D	49. D	64. C
5. D	20. A	35. D	50. A	65. A
6. D	21. D	36. D	51. A	66. B
7. A	22. C	37. A	52. A	67. B
8. B	23. D	38. B	53. D	68. C
9. D	24. D	39. A	54. C	69. B
10. B	25. A	40. D	55. C	70. B
11. C	26. B	41. A	56. B	71. C
12. C	27. B	42. D	57. B	72. D
13. C	28. B	43. D	58. B	73. B
14. D	29. B	44. A	59. D	74. A
15. A	30. B	45. C	60. B	75. A

TEST 2

DIRECTIONS: Each question or incomplete statement is followed by several suggested answers or completions. Select the one the BEST answers the question or completes the statement. *PRINT THE LETTER OF THE CORRECT ANSWER IN THE SPACE AT THE RIGHT.*

1. An 18-year-old girl is brought into a hospital emergency room by her family, who reported that she experienced sudden blindness. She had been arguing with her mother about why her mother was so much stricter with her than her father, when her mother suddenly blurted out that she and the father were seeking a divorce. The girl continued to argue for several minutes but then suddenly stopped and announced that she couldn't see anything. An examination reveals no neurological deficits. The client should most likely receive a diagnosis of   1.____

    A. conversion disorder
    B. somatoform disorder, not otherwise specified
    C. dissociative disorder
    D. hypochondriasis

2. An important difference between brief psychotherapy and crisis intervention is that   2.____

    A. brief therapy focuses on pathology
    B. crisis intervention focuses on specific issues
    C. brief therapy focuses on specific issues
    D. crisis intervention focuses on pathology

3. During an evaluation session in which the supervisor and practitioner are discussing the progress of the practitioner's current caseload, the practitioner admits to being unhappy with the overall progress of his clients, but attributes it to problems he has been experiencing because of excessive pressure placed on him by the supervisor. At this point in the evaluation, the supervisor should   3.____

    A. reassure the practitioner that whatever pressures have been placed on him have been for the benefit of his professional development
    B. apologize and suggest that the practitioner think of ways in which the supervisory relationship can be made more comfortable
    C. try to steer the focus of the discussion toward client progress
    D. remind the practitioner that he is the one ultimately responsible for handling the pressures that come with social work practice

4. In the time series design of program evaluation, the primary threat to internal validity is   4.____

    A. history
    B. selection
    C. testing
    D. regression to the mean

5. A client tells her clinician that members of an international espionage ring are after her to torture her and find out what she knows. She suspects that there are higher forces at work behind her persecution, but she can't tell the clinician what these forces are. Her beliefs have interfered with her work and social life for more than a year. The most appropriate diagnosis for this client is   5.____

A. psychotic disorder, not otherwise specified
B. schizophrenia, paranoid type
C. delusional disorder
D. schizoaffective disorder

6. Which of the following factors is NOT typically associated with ethnicity?

   A. Language
   B. Physical type
   C. Economic status
   D. Culture

7. A 19-year-old male client's father calls the social worker and requests information about his son's treatment. In this situation, the social worker should

   A. confirm that the son is in treatment but give no other information
   B. tell the father about his son's progress but not reveal any specifics
   C. set up a conjoint therapy session
   D. refuse to reveal any information

8. In an approach-avoidance conflict, as the person nears the goal,

   A. attraction and aversion both increase
   B. attraction and aversion both decrease
   C. attraction increases and aversion decreases
   D. atraction decreases and aversion increases

9. According the Herzberg's model of employee motivation, which of the following is a "hygiene" factor?

   A. Potential for growth
   B. Interesting, challenging work
   C. Freedom
   D. Salary

10. A disturbance of consciousness accompanied by some changes in cognition is the distinguishing feature of

    A. schizophrenia
    B. dementia
    C. delusion
    D. delirium

11. Public and private social service agencies generally differ in each of the following ways, EXCEPT

    A. practitioner certification requirements
    B. philosophy of service
    C. service eligibility requirements
    D. scope of services

12. Consistently, an employee is observed to be extremely friendly toward his boss, whom he really despises. From a Freudian perspective, the employee is exhibiting

A. reaction formation
B. isolation of affect
C. projection
D. sublimation

13. The purpose of an explanatory design for practice evaluation is to

    A. determine the causes of specific client behaviors
    B. examine and reflect on the intervention being used
    C. examine the impact of the intervention on the target behavior
    D. monitor client progress

14. Which of the following neurotransmitters or neuropeptides is generally deficient in clients with anorexia nervosa?

    A. Serotonin
    B. Cholecystokinin
    C. Dopamine
    D. Neuropeptide Y

15. Services that are provided to clients without a means test are described as

    A. pro-rated
    B. contributory
    C. eclectic
    D. universal

16. In a family intervention formed in the strategic model, a clinician who uses a "restraining strategy" will begin the intervention by

    A. warning the family of the danger of continuing its symptomatic behavior
    B. directing the family to stop its symptomatic behavior
    C. warning the family of the negative consequences of behavioral change
    D. instructing the family to engage in only nonsymptomatic behavior

17. The primary disadvantage associated with purchase-of-service agreements in social services is

    A. higher agency costs
    B. further fragmentation of the social service system
    C. decreased innovation in problem-solving
    D. diminished scope of services

18. Roles in the alcoholic family system have been labeled by Wegscheider and others. Typically, the youngest child in an alcoholic family occupies the role of

    A. mascot
    B. lost child
    C. hero
    D. scapegoat

19. The primary purpose for using confrontation in a client interview is to

A. teach mediation and conflict resolution skills
B. activate the client's potential for change
C. identify mixed messages in behaviors and thoughts or feelings
D. identify the processes the client uses to make changes

20. A clinician at a mental health clinic decides to work from the perspective of Rogers client-centered therapy. If the counselor goes against the policy of the clinic and decides to reject the use of diagnosis, it will be because from the person-centered perspective,

    A. the validity of diagnostic labels has not been empirically demonstrated
    B. diagnosis forces the therapist, rather than the client, to assume the expert role
    C. labeling results in an incongruence between self and experience
    D. labeling discourages the process of in-depth interpretation of the client's behavior

21. Which of the following interventions is one of the most frequently used therapies in the treatment of phobias?

    A. Exposure therapy
    B. Object relations
    C. Extinction
    D. Social skills training

22. Which of the following statements about therapeutic group composition is generally FALSE?

    A. Task groups that are homogeneous are less productive and cohesive than heterogeneous groups.
    B. Homogeneous groups of task-oriented, high-structure, impersonal people function as effective, change-producing human relations groups.
    C. Heterogeneous encounter groups are more effective in producing greater self-actualization of members.
    D. Homogeneous groups of person-oriented, low-structure people do not generally function as effective human relations groups.

23. When behaviors are known and categorized prior to an observation, and the intention is to collect quantitative data, the method of choice is

    A. structured observation
    B. the Likert scale
    C. participant observation
    D. structured interview

24. A client who was abused as a child, whenever speaking of her parents, tends to cast the father in the most negative light possible, describing his as evil and every encounter with him as a disaster. Of her mother, however, she has only the most glowing praise, often referring to her as a saint. From a psychodynamic perspective, the client is using the defense mechanism known as

    A. reaction formation
    B. primitive idealization
    C. projection
    D. splitting

25. In the transactional analysis model of social intercourse, the safest type of interaction is

   A. a game
   B. intimate
   C. ritualistic
   D. a pastime

26. Dissociative amnesia is usually
   I. related to the inability to recall important personal information
   II. retrograde
   III. selective
   IV. accompanied by apraxia

   A. I and II
   B. II and III
   C. I, II and III
   D. II, III and IV

27. People often have difficulty receiving information because of an impairment or other barrier. Which of these will probably NOT help such a person to better understand a message?

   A. Repeating the message
   B. Changing the sequence of the message
   C. Changing the form in which the message is transmitted
   D. Using an interpreter

28. A social worker is working with an autistic child who is mute. The major goal of intervention is the development of language. The social worker begins by rewarding the child with food whenever he vocalizes. The social worker then begins to reward the child only when his vocalizations occur within ten seconds of the social worker's vocalization, then only if the child's vocalizations resemble the social worker's, and so on, until the child's vocalizations are identical to those of the social worker. The technique is used until the child is eventually using words and sentences. This technique is known as:

   A. counterconditioning
   B. chaining
   C. shaping
   D. prompting

29. Potential limitations on confidentiality should be discussed with a client

   A. when the social worker determines it to be appropriate
   B. at the onset of the professional relationship
   C. at the onset of the professional relationship and thereafter as needed
   D. and documented in writing as soon as possible

30. Other than describing a client's problem in a way that imposes meaning on a large amount of information, the primary cognitive task of assessment is to

   A. establish client comfort with the therapeutic plan
   B. selectively focus on the information that will be most useful to the treatment planning process

C. infer whether a specific groups of facts or observations belongs to a larger known category of problems
D. identify the client's feelings of concern

31. The status of the practitioner/client therapeutic relationship is seen as an important aspect of therapy in each of the following models, EXCEPT

    A. ecosystems
    B. psychoanalysis
    C. client-centered
    D. behavioral

32. Among the skills important to effective communication with clients, the most sophisticated and complex is/are

    A. encouraging, paraphrasing, and summarization
    B. confrontation
    C. influencing skills
    D. open and closed questions

33. The _____ approach to human behavior attempts to describe behaviors in ways that allow for generalization across cultures.

    A. etic
    B. holistic
    C. emic
    D. pluralist

34. The most widely-used bivariate statistical measure in social work is

    A. regression analysis
    B. cross-tabulation
    C. slope/drift
    D. correlation

35. Which of the following statements is most abstract?

    A. Last night my mother told me I was a disappointment.
    B. I cry all day long. I can't eat.
    C. My daughter just sent me a letter.
    D. My family is very close.

36. Each of the following is viewed by clinicians as an important element of the therapeutic relationship, EXCEPT

    A. confidentiality
    B. dependability
    C. sympathy
    D. confidence

37. The _____ theory of human development holds that human behavior is strongly influenced by biology, is tied to evolution, and is characterized by critical and sensitive periods.

A. Biosocial
B. Ecological
C. Social learning
D. Ethological

38. The residual model of social welfare
    I. is developed piecemeal as a reaction to the development of social problems, rather than in anticipation of them
    II. views government as the last line of defense for people experiencing problems
    III. views family and work as the first line of defense
    IV. expects individuals to have trouble meeting the needs of modem living

    A. I only
    B. I and II
    C. I, II, and III
    D. I, II, III and IV

39. One of the helping models for multiproblem families is the Multiple-Impact Family-Therapy (MIFT) model, which includes each of the following elements, EXCEPT

    A. a long-term, client-centered approach
    B. an extended session format
    C. use of a team of professionals who work directly with the family
    D. immediate response to a request for service

40. Which of the following has NOT been a factor in the recent growth of the for-profit sector of social services in the United States?

    A. The ability of for-profit agencies to offer more stable financial sources of income than other investments
    B. The historical ability of private-sector solutions to solve problems that the government has failed to solve
    C. The growing complexity and number of problems experienced by the disadvantaged
    D. The existence of for-profit opportunities outside of public health insurance benefits

41. Which of the following is NOT typically a factor used by private clinicians to determine fees for clients?

    A. The amount charged by local psychiatrists of equal experience
    B. What the worker thinks will be the most attractive rate to the clientele she hopes to attract
    C. What third-party financing organizations identify as reasonable and customary charges
    D. How much other helping professionals charge for such services

42. Erikson's final stage of psychosocial development, experienced during late adulthood, is

    A. industry vs. inferiority
    B. generativity vs. stagnation
    C. intimacy vs. isolation
    D. integrity vs. despair

43. Which of the following approaches to social services policymaking assess the process of moving from the identification of a social problem to implementing a policy and assessing the impact the policy has on the original problem?

    A. Prescriptive
    B. Investment
    C. Cause and consequences
    D. Formative

44. Research suggests that negative emotional effects from divorce are LEAST likely to impact

    A. women who do not remarry
    B. women who remarry
    C. men who do not remarry
    D. men who remarry

45. Closed questions typically do NOT begin with the word

    A. how
    B. is
    C. do
    D. are

46. In order to receive a diagnosis of acute stress disorder that conforms to DSM-IV standards, a client's symptoms must occur within _____ of a traumatic event.

    A. 5 days
    B. 4 weeks
    C. 3 months
    D. 6 months

47. Which of the following types of programs is typically administered exclusively at the county level?

    A. Food stamps
    B. AFDC
    C. Medical assistance
    D. General assistance

48. In the clinical supervision of a social work practitioner, a good general policy is to

    A. begin with technical skill learning and then move to theoretical and perspective learning
    B. begin with perspective learning and then move to technical skill learning
    C. teach a supervisee technical skills and theory simultaneously
    D. avoid both technical skills and theory and instead focus on smaller, concrete problems faced by the practitioner

49. Approximately what percentage of child maltreatment/abuse cases involve sexual abuse?

    A. 5   B. 10   C. 30   D. 50

50. In the United States, most social policy is formulated

    A. by individual agency boards
    B. in a de facto manner by the direct practice of social workers
    C. through legislation
    D. by state boards

51. Which of the following terms is used to describe memory loss that has a purely psychological cause?

    A. Anterograde
    B. Organic
    C. Retrograde
    D. Inorganic

52. Which of the following statements reveals a client with a sensorimotor emotional orientation?

    A. A lot of us are angry. I know my boss is busy, but his forgetting to sign the payroll is going to cost some of us our weekend plans.
    B. I'm feeling lost I start to tremble when I go out in public.
    C. It seems that every time my wife is late meeting me somewhere, I get really angry with her. My time is valuable.
    D. I feel really angry because my best friend borrowed my car without asking.

53. In order to receive a diagnosis of adjustment disorder that conforms to DSM-IV standards, a client's symptoms must occur within _____ of a traumatic event

    A. 5 days
    B. 4 weeks
    C. 3 months
    D. 6 months

54. In the static-group comparison design of program evaluation, the primary threat to external validity is

    A. maturation-treatment interaction
    B. selection-treatment interaction
    C. reactive effects
    D. history-treatment interaction

55. According to Ainsworth, a "Type B" baby

    A. exhibits insecurity by avoiding the mother
    B. exhibits insecurity by resisting the mother
    C. exhibits insecurity by clinging to the mother
    D. uses the mother as a secure base from which to explore the environment

56. Which of the following is a primary social work setting?

A. Community center
B. Child protective services agency
C. Hospital
D. Nursing home

57. A client is a 40-year-old man who works as a night custodian at a local bank building. He keeps to himself and seems to have no interests outside his job, his stamp collection, and his two cats. He lives alone in a small apartment, has no close friends, and appears to have to interest in making friends. If this client is to receive a DSM-IV diagnosis, what would it be?

    A. Avoidant personality disorder
    B. Schizoid personality disorder
    C. Antisocial personality disorder
    D. No diagnosis—the man's isolation is not a disorder

58. A social or financial service that requires an applicant to prove financial need in order to receive the service is described as

    A. means-tested
    B. prescriptive
    C. residual
    D. eclectic

59. The initial aim in treating a client with conversion disorder is

    A. removal of the symptom
    B. determining predisposing factors
    C. forming a description of interpersonal relationships
    D. discovering precipitating stressors

60. Which of the following is NOT a preexperimental design for program evaluation?

    A. One-group pretest/posttest
    B. Client satisfaction surveys
    C. Static-group comparison
    D. Solomon four-group approach

61. In their definition of "family," many Asian Americans, especially Chinese Americans, are likely to include
    I. members of the nuclear family
    II. members of the extended family
    III. the informal network of community relations
    IV. all their ancestors and descendants

    A. I and II
    B. I, II and III
    C. I, II and IV
    D. I, II, III and IV

62. Within the context of the therapeutic relationship, practitioners and clients deal either explicitly or implicitly with
    I. past experiences that have affected abilities to relate to others
    II. the present physical, emotional, and perceptual state of the transaction
    III. each person's expectations of the process

    A. I only
    B. I and II
    C. II and III
    D. I, II and II

63. Assertiveness and social skills training are interventions MOST likely to be useful to clients with

    A. panic disorder with agoraphobia
    B. avoidant personality disorder
    C. narcissistic personality disorder
    D. schizoid personality disorder

64. A client reports to a practitioner at an outpatient care clinic in clear psychological distress, exhibiting paranoia and severe anxiety. The clinician is certain that the client has some form of anxiety disorder. The patient has severe liver disease, but the clinician can't determine whether this is a factor; it's possible that the problem is related to other factors such as the client's persistent substance abuse. The most likely DSM-IV diagnosis would be Anxiety Disorder,

    A. provisional
    B. not otherwise specified
    C. with generalized anxiety
    D. undifferentiated

65. Which of the following is NOT generally a guideline for supervisors to follow regarding case presentation?

    A. The presentation should be organized around questions to be answered.
    B. The supervisor should present a case first.
    C. The presentation should progress from practitioner dynamics to client dynamics.
    D. The presentation should be based on written or audiovisual material.

66. A thirty-five-year-old client was referred by a friend because of her sadness and talk of suicide, which were brought on by the death of her lover several years ago but never fully subsided. A practitioner working from the existential viewpoint would view the goal of assessment with this client as

    A. an in-depth understanding of her subjective experience
    B. identifying the support resources already available to her
    C. the identification of situations and stimuli that reinforce her depressive responses
    D. achieving transference

67. Which of the following processes typically occurs LATEST in the therapeutic relationship?

    A. Individuation
    B. Idealization

C. Individualization
D. Identification

68. A social worker has been seeing a client who whose wife left him and moved out of state with the children. During a session, the client says he wishes he could find out where she lives, so he could make her pay for what she's done. The social worker should

    A. call domestic violence experts and document the statement
    B. call domestic violence experts and get legal advice
    C. call the police
    D. try to find the ex-wife and warn her

68.____

69. Some Marxist-oriented behavioral theorists believe that when individuals meet in face-to-face encounters, they make several different adaptations. For example, when individuals of different classes meet, the interaction tends to be very narrow and role-prescribed. This is an example of _____ generalization.

    A. means-end
    B. feelings
    C. control-purposiveness
    D. detachment

69.____

70. A practitioner using rational-emotive therapy to help a child who is depressed has gathered information from the child's parents and teachers, and has collected formal assessment instruments that were completed by the parents and the child. The practitioner then meets with the parents and the child together, and asks the parents a series of questions about their child's symptoms and their history of attempts to deal with the problem. The practitioner's NEXT step should be to

    A. question both the parents and the child about treatment goals
    B. assess the parents and the child for secondary disturbance
    C. ask for the child's opinion of her parents' statements
    D. assess the practical and/or emotional problems presented

70.____

71. The record-keeping requirements at a typical social services agency require the completion of progress notes at an interval no longer than

    A. after every client contact
    B. weekly
    C. every 30 days
    D. every 90 days

71.____

72. NASW policy regarding foster care and transracial adoption states that placement decisions should reflect a child's need for

    A. basic material comforts
    B. continuity
    C. ethnic/racial integrity
    D. a stimulating, challenging environment

72.____

73. Which of the following statements about the behavioral approach to treatment is FALSE?

73.____

A. Behavioral interventions are intended to modify only certain, limited aspects of human behavior
B. Under certain conditions, behaviorists are concerned with affect and cognitions
C. Behaviorists prefer observation over introspection
D. Behaviorists believe that a client's symptoms are merely observable behaviors that have been labeled as problematic

74. Within the family life-cycle perspective, divorces are sometimes referred to as   74._____

    A. derailments
    B. dislocations
    C. non-normative crises
    D. ruptures

75. Which of the following statements is TRUE regarding summative program evaluations?   75._____

    A. Interpretive approaches using qualitative data are particularly useful.
    B. They make no attempt to determine causality.
    C. Validity is a central concern.
    D. Evaluations provide detail about a program's strengths and weaknesses.

KEY (CORRECT ANSWERS)

1. A	16. C	31. D	46. B	61. C
2. A	17. B	32. C	47. D	62. D
3. C	18. A	33. A	48. A	63. B
4. A	19. B	34. B	49. B	64. B
5. B	20. B	35. D	50. C	65. C
6. C	21. A	36. C	51. A	66. A
7. D	22. A	37. D	52. B	67. A
8. A	23. A	38. C	53. C	68. B
9. D	24. D	39. A	54. B	69. A
10. D	25. C	40. C	55. D	70. C
11. A	26. C	41. A	56. B	71. C
12. A	27. B	42. D	57. B	72. B
13. C	28. C	43. C	58. A	73. A
14. C	29. C	44. A	59. A	74. B
15. D	30. C	45. A	60. D	75. C

PREPARING WRITTEN MATERIAL

PARAGRAPH REARRANGEMENT
COMMENTARY

The sentences that follow are in scrambled order. You are to rearrange them in proper order and indicate the letter choice containing the correct answer at the space at the right.

Each group of sentences in this section is actually a paragraph presented in scrambled order. Each sentence in the group has a place in that paragraph; no sentence is to be left out. You are to read each group of sentences and decide upon the best order in which to put the sentences so as to form a well-organized paragraph.

The questions in this section measure the ability to solve a problem when all the facts relevant to its solution are not given.

More specifically, certain positions of responsibility and authority require the employee to discover connection between events sometimes, apparently, unrelated. In order to do this, the employee will find it necessary to correctly infer that unspecified events have probably occurred or are likely to occur. This ability becomes especially important when action must be taken on incomplete information.

Accordingly, these questions require competitors to choose among several suggested alternatives, each of which presents a different sequential arrangement of the events. Competitors must choose the MOST logical of the suggested sequences.

In order to do so, they may be required to draw on general knowledge to infer missing concepts or events that are essential to sequencing the given events. Competitors should be careful to infer only what is essential to the sequence. The plausibility of the wrong alternatives will always require the inclusion of unlikely events or of additional chains of events which are NOT essential to sequencing the given events.

It's very important to remember that you are looking for the best of the four possible choices, and that the best choice of all may not even be one of the answers you're given to choose from.

There is no one right way to solve these problems. Many people have found it helpful to first write out the order of the sentences, as they would have arranged them, on their scrap paper before looking at the possible answers. If their optimum answer is there, this can save them some time. If it isn't, this method can still give insight into solving the problem. Others find it most helpful to just go through each of the possible choices, contrasting each as they go along. You should use whatever method feels comfortable and works for you.

While most of these types of questions are not that difficult, we've added a higher percentage of the difficult type, just to give you more practice. Usually there are only one or two questions on this section that contain such subtle distinctions that you're unable to answer confidently. And you then may find yourself stuck deciding between two possible choices, neither of which you're sure about.

EXAMINATION SECTION
TEST 1

DIRECTIONS: The following groups of sentences need to be arranged in an order that makes sense. Select the letter preceding the sequence that represents the BEST sentence order. *PRINT THE LETTER OF THE CORRECT ANSWER IN THE SPACE AT THE RIGHT.*

1. I. The keyboard was purposely designed to be a little awkward to slow typists down.
    II. The arrangement of letters on the keyboard of a typewriter was not designed for the convenience of the typist.
    III. Fortunately, no one is suggesting that a new keyboard be designed right away.
    IV. If one were, we would have to learn to type all over again.
    V. The reason was that the early machines were slower than the typists and would jam easily.
    The CORRECT answer is:
    A. I, III, IV, II, V
    B. II, V, I, IV, III
    C. V, I, II, III, IV
    D. II, I, V, III, IV

    1.____

2. I. The majority of the new service jobs are part-time or low-paying.
    II. According to the U.S. Bureau of Labor Statistics, jobs in the service sector constitute 72% of all jobs in this country.
    III. If more and more workers receive less and less money, who will buy the goods and services needed to keep the economy going?
    IV. The service sector is by far the fastest growing part of the United States economy.
    V. Some economists look upon this trend with great concern.
    The CORRECT answer is:
    A. II, IV, I, V, III
    B. II, III, IV, I, V
    C. V, IV, II, III, I
    D. III, I, II, IV, V

    2.____

3. I. They can also affect one's endurance.
    II. This can stabilize blood sugar levels, and ensure that the brain is receiving a steady, constant, supply of glucose, so that one is *hitting on all cylinders* while taking the test.
    III. By food, we mean real food, not junk food or unhealthy snacks.
    IV. For this reason, it is important not to skip a meal, and to bring food with you to the exam.
    V. One's blood sugar levels can affect how clearly one is able to think and concentrate during an exam.
    The CORRECT answer is:
    A. V, IV, II, III, I
    B. V, II, I, IV, III
    C. V, I, IV, III, II
    D. V, IV, I, III, II

    3.____

4. I. Those who are the embodiment of desire are absorbed in material quests, and those who are the embodiment of feeling are warriors who value power more than possession.
    II. These qualities are in everyone, but in different degrees.
    III. But those who value understanding yearn not for goods or victory, but for knowledge.
    IV. According to Plato, human behavior flows from three main sources: desire, emotion, and knowledge.
    V. In the perfect state, the industrial forces would produce but not rule, the military would protect but not rule, and the forces of knowledge, the philosopher kings, would reign.
    The CORRECT answer is:
    A. IV, V, I, II, III
    B. V, I, II, III, IV
    C. IV, III, II, I, V
    D. IV, II, I, III, V

5. I. Of the more than 26,000 tons of garbage produced daily in New York City, 12,000 tons arrive daily at Fresh Kills.
    II. In a month, enough garbage accumulates there to fill the Empire State Building.
    III. In 1937, the Supreme Court halted the practice of dumping the trash of New York City into the sea.
    IV. Although the garbage is compacted, in a few years the mounds of garbage at Fresh Kills will be the highest points south of Maine's Mount Desert Island on the Eastern Seaboard.
    V. Instead, tugboats now pull barges of much of the trash to Staten Island and the largest landfill in the world, Fresh Kills.
    The CORRECT answer is:
    A. III, V, IV, I, II
    B. III, V, II, IV, I
    C. III, V, I, II, IV
    D. III, II, V, IV, I

6. I. Communists rank equality very high, but freedom very low.
    II. Unlike communists, conservatives place a high value on freedom and a very low value on equality.
    III. A recent study demonstrated that one way to classify people's political beliefs is to look at the importance placed on two words: freedom and equality.
    IV. Thus, by demonstrating how members of these groups feel about the two words, the study has proved to be useful for political analysts in several European countries.
    V. According to the study, socialists and liberals rank both freedom and equality very high, while fascists rate both very low.
    The CORRECT answer is:
    A. III, V, I, II, IV
    B. V, IV, III, I, II
    C. III, V, IV, II, I
    D. III, I, II, IV, V

7. I. "Can there be anything more amazing than this?"
    II. If the riddle is successfully answered, his dead brothers will be brought back to life.
    III. "Even though man sees those around him dying every day," says Dharmaraj, "he still believes and acts as if he were immortal."
    IV. "What is the cause of ceaseless wonder?" asks the Lord of the Lake.
    V. In the ancient epic, The Mahabharata, a riddle is asked of one of the Pandava brothers.
    The CORRECT answer is:
    A. V, II, I, IV, III
    B. V, IV, III, I, II
    C. V, II, IV, III, I
    D. V, II, IV, I, III

7._____

8. I. On the contrary, the two main theories—the cooperative (neoclassical) theory and the radical (labor theory)—clearly rest on very different assumptions, which have very different ethical overtones.
    II. The distribution of income is the primary factor in determining the relative levels of material well-being that different groups or individuals attain.
    III. Of all issues in economics, the distribution of income is one of the most controversial.
    IV. The neoclassical theory tends to support the existing income distribution (or minor changes), while the labor theory ends to support substantial changes in the way income is distributed.
    V. The intensity of the controversy reflects the fact that different economic theories are not purely neutral, *detached* theories with no ethical or moral implications.
    The CORRECT answer is:
    A. II, I, V, IV, III
    B. III, II, V, I, IV
    C. III, V, II, I, IV
    D. III, V, IV, I, II

8._____

9. I. The pool acts as a broker and ensures that the cheapest power gets used first.
    II. Every six seconds, the pool's computer monitors all of the generating stations in the state and decides which to ask for more power and which to cut back.
    III. The buying and selling of electrical power is handled by the New York Power Pool in Guilderland, New York.
    IV. This is to the advantage of both the buying and selling utilities.
    V. The pool began operation in 1970, and consists of the state's eight electric utilities.
    The CORRECT answer is:
    A. V, I, II, III, IV
    B. IV, II, I, III, V
    C. III, V, I, IV, II
    D. V, III, IV, II, I

9._____

10. I. Modern English is much simpler grammatically than Old English.
    II. Finnish grammar is very complicated; there are some fifteen cases, for example.
    III. Chinese, a very old language, may seem to be the exception, but it is the great number of characters/words that must be mastered that makes it so difficult to learn, not its grammar.
    IV. The newest literary language—that is, written as well as spoken—is Finish, whose literary roots go back only to about the middle of the nineteenth century.
    V. Contrary to popular belief, the longer a language is been in use the simpler its grammar—not the reverse.

    The CORRECT answer is:
    A. IV, I, II, III, V
    B. V, I, IV, II, III
    C. I, II, IV, III, V
    D. IV, II, III, I, V

10.____

KEY (CORRECT ANSWERS)

1.	D	6.	A
2.	A	7.	C
3.	C	8.	B
4.	D	9.	C
5.	C	10.	B

TEST 2

DIRECTIONS: This type of question tests your ability to recognize accurate paraphrasing, well-constructed paragraphs, and appropriate style and tone. It is important that the answer you select contains only the facts or concepts given in the original sentences. It is also important that you be aware of incomplete sentences, inappropriate transitions, unsupported opinions, incorrect usage, and illogical sentence order. Paragraphs that do not include all the necessary facts and concepts, that distort them, or that add new ones are not considered correct.

The format for this section may vary. Sometimes, long paragraphs are given, and emphasis is placed on style and organization. Our first five questions are of this type. Other times, the paragraphs are shorter, and there is less emphasis on style and more emphasis on accurate representation of information. Our second group of five questions are of this nature.

For each of Questions 1 through 10, select the paragraph that BEST expresses the ideas contained in the sentences above it. *PRINT THE LETTER OF THE CORRECT ANSWER IN THE SPACE AT THE RIGHT.*

1. I. Listening skills are very important for managers.
    II. Listening skills are not usually emphasized.
    III. Whenever managers are depicted in books, manuals or the media, they are always talking, never listening.
    IV. We'd like you to read the enclosed handout on listening skills and to try to consciously apply them this week.
    V. We guarantee they will improve the quality of your interactions.

    A. Unfortunately, listening skills are not usually emphasized for managers. Managers are always depicted as talking, never listening. We'd like you to read the enclosed handout on listening skills. Please try to apply these principles this week. If you do, we guarantee they will improve the quality of your interactions.
    B. The enclosed handout on listening skills will be important improving the quality of your interactions. We guarantee it. All you have to do is take sometime this week to read and to consciously try to apply the principles. Listening skills are very important for manages, but they are not usually emphasized. Whenever managers are depicted in books, manuals or the media, they are always talking, never listening.
    C. Listening well is one of the most important skills a manager can have, yet it's not usually given much attention. Think about any representation of managers in books, manuals, or in the media that you may have seen. They're always talking, never listening. We'd like you to read the enclosed handout on listening skills and consciously try to apply them the rest of the week. We guarantee you will see a difference in the quality of your interactions.

1.____

123

D. Effective listening, one very important tool in the effective manager's arsenal, is usually not emphasized enough. The usual depiction of managers in books, manuals or the media is one in which they are always talking, never listening. We'd like you to read the enclosed handout and consciously try to apply the information contained therein throughout the rest of the week. We feel sure that you will see a marked difference in the quality of your interactions.

2. I. Chekhov wrote three dramatic masterpieces which share certain themes and formats: Uncle Vanya, The Cherry Orchard, and The Three Sisters.
    II. They are primarily concerned with the passage of time and how this erodes human aspirations.
    III. The plays are haunted by the ghosts of the wasted life.
    IV. The characters are concerned with life's lesser problems; however, such as the inability to make decisions, loyalty to the wrong cause, and the inability to be clear.
    V. This results in sweet, almost aching, type of a sadness referred to as Chekhovian.

2.____

    A. Chekhov wrote three dramatic masterpieces: Uncle Vanya, The Cherry Orchard, and The Three Sisters. These masterpieces share certain themes and formats: the passage of time, how time erodes human aspirations, and the ghosts of wasted life. Each masterpiece is characterized by a sweet, almost aching, type of sadness that has become known as Chekhovian. The sweetness of this sadness hinges on the fact that it is not the great tragedies of life which are destroying these characters, but their minor flaws: indecisiveness, misplaced loyalty, unclarity.

    B. The Cherry Orchard, Uncle Vanya, and The Three Sisters are three dramatic masterpieces written by Chekhov that use similar formats to explore a common theme. Each is primarily concerned with the way that passing time wears down human aspirations, and each is haunted by the ghosts of the wasted life. The characters are shown struggling futilely with the lesser problems of life: indecisiveness, loyalty to the wrong cause, and the inability to be clear. These struggles create a mood of sweet, almost aching, sadness that has become known as Chekhovian.

    C. Chekhov's dramatic masterpieces are, along with The Cherry Orchard, Uncle Vanya, and The Three Sisters. These plays share certain thematic and formal similarities. They are concerned most of all with the passage of time and the way in which time erodes human aspirations. Each play is haunted by the specter of the wasted life. Chekhov's characters are caught, however, by life's lesser snares: indecisiveness, loyalty to the wrong cause, and unclarity. The characteristic mood is a sweet, almost aching type of sadness that has come to be known as Chekhovian.

    D. A Chekhovian mood is characterized by sweet, almost aching, sadness. The term comes from three dramatic tragedies by Chekhov which revolve around the sadness of a wasted life. The three masterpieces (Uncle Vanya, The Three Sisters, and The Cherry Orchard) share the same theme and format. The plays are concerned with how the passage of time erodes human aspirations. They are peopled with characters who are struggling with life's lesser problems. These are people who are indecisive, loyal to the wrong causes, or are unable to make themselves clear.

3.
I. Movie previews have often helped producers decide which parts of movies they should take out or leave in.
II. The first 1933 preview of King Kong was very helpful to the producers because many people ran screaming from the theater and would not return when four men first attacked by Kong were eaten by giant spiders.
III. The 1950 premiere of Sunset Boulevard resulted in the filming of an entirely new beginning, and a delay of six months in the film's release.
IV. In the original opening scene, William Holden was in a morgue talking with thirty-six other "corpses" about the ways some of them had died.
V. When he began to tell them of his life with Gloria Swanson, the audience found this hilarious, instead of taking the scene seriously.

3.____

A. Movie previews have often helped producers decide what parts of movies they should leave in or take out. For example, the first preview of King Kong in 1933 was very helpful. In one scene, four men were first attacked by Kong and then eaten by giant spiders. Many members of the audience ran screaming from the theater and would not return. The premiere of the 1950 film Sunset Boulevard was also very helpful. In the original opening scene, William Holden was in a morgue with thirty-six other "corpses," discussing the ways some of them had died. When he began to tell them of his life with Gloria Swanson, the audience found this hilarious. They were supposed to take the scene seriously. The result was a delay of six months in the release of the film while a new beginning was added.

B. Movie previews have often helped producers decide whether they should change various parts of a movie. After the 1933 preview of King Kong, a scene in which four men who had been attacked by Kong were eaten by giant spiders was taken out as many people ran screaming from the theater and would not return. The 1950 premiere of Sunset Boulevard also led to some changes. In the original opening scene, William Holden was in a morgue talking with thirty-six other "corpses" about the ways some of them had died. When he began to tell them of his life with Gloria Swanson, the audience found this hilarious, instead of taking the scene seriously.

C. What do Sunset Boulevard and King Kong have in common? Both show the value of using movie previews to test audience reaction. The first 1933 preview of King Kong showed that a scene showing four men being eaten by giant spiders after having been attacked by Kong was too frightening for many people. They ran screaming from the theater and couldn't be coaxed back. The 1950 premiere of Sunset Boulevard was also a scream, but not the kind the producers intended. The movie opens with William Holden lying in a morgue discussing the ways they had died with thirty-six other "corpses." When he began to tell them of his life with Gloria Swanson, the audience couldn't take him seriously. Their laughter caused a six-month delay while the beginning was rewritten.

D. Producers very often use movie previews to decide if changes are needed. The premiere of Sunset Boulevard in 1950 led to a new beginning and a six-month delay in film release. At the beginning, William Holden and thirty-six other "corpses" discuss the ways some of them died. Rather than taking this seriously, the audience thought it was hilarious when he began to tell them of his life with Gloria Swanson. The first 1933 preview of King Kong was very helpful for its producers because one scene so terrified the audience that many of them ran screaming from the theater and would not return. In this particular scene, four men who had first been attacked by Kong were eaten by giant spiders.

4. I. It is common for supervisors to view employees as "things" to be manipulated.   4.____
    II. This approach does not motivate employees, nor does the carrot-and-stick approach because employees often recognize these behaviors and resent them.
    III. Supervisors can change these behaviors by using self-inquiry and persistence.
    IV. The best managers genuinely respect those they work with, are supportive and helpful, and are interested in working as a team with those they supervise.
    V. They disagree with the Golden Rule that says "he or she who has the gold makes the rules."

    A. Some managers act as if they think the Golden Rule means "he or she who has the gold makes the rules." They show disrespect to employees by seeing them as "things" to be manipulated. Obviously, this approach does not motivate employees any more than the carrot-and-stick approach motivates them. The employees are smart enough to spot these behaviors and resent them. On the other hand, the managers genuinely respect those they work with, are supportive and helpful, and are interested in working as a team. Self-inquiry and persistence can change even the former type of supervisor into the latter.
    B. Many supervisors all into the trap of viewing employees as "things" to be manipulated, or try to motivate them by using a carrot-and-stick approach. These methods do not motivate employees, who often recognize the behaviors and resent them. Supervisors can change these behaviors, however, by using self-inquiry and persistence. The best managers are supportive and helpful, and have genuine respect for those with whom they work. They are interested in working as a team with those they supervise. To them, the Golden Rule is not "he or she who has the gold makes the rules."
    C. Some supervisors see employees as "things" to be used or manipulated using a carrot-and-stick technique. These methods don't work. Employees often see through them and resent them. A supervisor who

wants to change may do so. The techniques of self-inquiry and persistence can be used to turn him or her into the type of supervisor who doesn't think the Golden Rule is "he or she who has the gold makes the rules." They may become like the best managers who treat those with whom they work with respect and give them help and support. These are the manager who know how to build a team.

D. Unfortunately, many supervisors act as if their employees are objects whose movements they can position at will. This mistaken belief has the same result as another popular motivational technique—the carrot-and-stick approach. Both attitudes can lead to the same result—resentment from those employees who recognize the behaviors for what they are. Supervisors who recognize these behaviors can change through the use of persistence and the use of self-inquiry. It's important to remember that the best managers respect their employees. They readily give necessary help and support and are interested in working as a team with those they supervise. To these managers, the Golden Rule is not "he or she who has the gold makes the rules."

5.
I. The first half of the nineteenth century produced a group of pessimistic poets—Byron, De Musset, Heine, Pushkin, and Leopardi.
II. It also produced a group of pessimistic composers—Schubert, Chopin, Schumann, and even the later Beethoven.
III. Above all, in philosophy, there was the profoundly pessimistic philosopher, Schopenhauer.
IV. The Revolution was dead, the Bourbons were restored, the feudal barons were reclaiming their land, and progress everywhere was being suppressed, as the great age was over.
V. "I thank God," said Goethe, "that I am not young in so thoroughly finished a world."

5._____

A. "I thank God," said Goethe, "that I am not young in so thoroughly finished a world." The Revolution was dead, the Bourbons were restored, the feudal barons were reclaiming their land, and progress everywhere was being suppressed. The first half of the nineteenth century produced a group of pessimistic poets: Byron, De Musset, Heine, Pushkin, and Leopardi. It also produced pessimistic composers: Schubert, Chopin, Schumann. Although Beethoven came later, he fits into this group, too. Finally and above all, it also produced a profoundly pessimistic philosopher, Schopenhauer. The great age was over.

B. The first half of the nineteenth century produced a group of pessimistic poets: Byron, De Musset, Heine, Pushkin, and Leopardi. It produced a group of pessimistic composers: Schubert, Chopin, Schumann, and even the later Beethoven. Above all, it produced a profoundly pessimistic philosopher, Schopenhauer. For each of these men, the great age was over. The Revolution was dead, and the Bourbons were restored. The feudal barons were reclaiming their land, and progress everywhere was being suppressed.

C. The great age was over. The Revolution was dead—the Bourbons were restored, and the feudal barons were reclaiming their land. Progress everywhere was being suppressed. Out of this climate came a profound pessimism. Poets, like Byron, De Musset, Heine, Pushkin, and Leopardi; composers, like Schubert, Chopin, Schumann, and even the later Beethoven; and above all, a profoundly pessimistic philosopher, Schopenauer. This pessimism which arose in the first half of the nineteenth century is illustrated by these words of Goethe, "I thank God that I am not young in so thoroughly finished a world."

D. The first half of the nineteenth century produced a group of pessimistic poets, Byron, De Musset, Heine, Pushkin, and Leopardi—and a group of pessimistic composers, Schubert, Chopin, Schumann, and the later Beethoven. Above it all, it produced a profoundly pessimistic philosopher, Schopenhauer. The great age was over. The Revolution was dead, the Bourbons were restored, the feudal barons were reclaiming their land, and progress everywhere was being suppressed. "I thank God," said Goethe, "that I am not young in so thoroughly finished a world."

6. I. A new manager sometimes may feel insecure about his or her competence in the new position.
    II. The new manager may then exhibit defensive or arrogant behavior towards those one supervises, or the new manager may direct overly flattering behavior toward one's new supervisor.

    A. Sometimes, a new manager may feel insecure about his or her ability to perform well in this new position. The insecurity may lead him or her to treat others differently. He or she may display arrogant or defensive behavior towards those he or she supervises, or be overly flattering to his or her new supervisor.
    B. A new manager may sometimes feel insecure about his or her ability to perform well in the new position. He or she may then become arrogant, defensive, or overly flattering towards those he or she works with.
    C. There are times when a new manager may be insecure about how well he or she can perform in the new job. The new manager may also behave defensive or act in an arrogant way towards those he or she supervises, or overly flatter his or her boss.
    D. Sometimes a new manager may feel insecure about his or her ability to perform well in the new position. He or she may then display arrogant or defensive behavior towards those they supervise, or become overly flattering towards their supervisors.

6._____

7. I. It is possible to eliminate unwanted behavior by bringing it under stimulus control—tying the behavior to a cue, and then never, or rarely, giving the cue.
    II. One trainer successfully used this method to keep an energetic young porpoise from coming out of her tank whenever she felt like it, which was potentially dangerous.
    III. Her trainer taught her to do it for a reward, in response to a hand signal, and then rarely gave the signal.

7._____

A. Unwanted behavior can be eliminated by tying the behavior to a cue, and then never, or rarely, giving the cue. This is called stimulus control. One trainer was able to use this method to keep an energetic young porpoise from coming out of her tank by teaching her to come out for a reward in response to a hand signal, and then rarely giving the signal.
B. Stimulus control can be used to eliminate unwanted behavior. In this method, behavior is tied to a cue, and then the cue is rarely, if ever, given. One trainer was able to successfully use stimulus control to keep an energetic young porpoise from coming out of her tank whenever she felt like it—a potentially dangerous practice. She taught the porpoise to come out for a reward when she gave a hand signal, and then rarely gave the signal.
C. It is possible to eliminate behavior that is undesirable by bringing it under stimulus control by tying behavior to a signal, and then rarely giving the signal. One trainer successfully used this method to keep an energetic porpoise from coming out of her tank, a potentially dangerous situation. Her trainer taught the porpoise to do it for a reward, in response to a hand signal, and then would rarely give the signal.
D. By using stimulus control, it is possible to eliminate unwanted behavior by tying the behavior to a cue, and then rarely or never give the cue. One trainer was able to use this method to successfully stop a young porpoise from coming out of her tank whenever she felt like it. To curb this potentially dangerous practice, the porpoise was taught by the trainer to come out of the tank for a reward, in response to a hand signal, and then rarely given the signal.

8. I. There is a great deal of concern over the safety of commercial trucks, caused by their greatly increased role in serious accidents since federal deregulation in 1981.
   II. Recently, 60 percent of trucks in New York and Connecticut and 70 percent of trucks in Maryland randomly stopped by state troopers failed safety inspections.
   III. Sixteen states in the United States require no training at all for truck drivers.

8.____

A. Since federal deregulation in 1981, there has been a great deal of concern over the safety of commercial trucks, and their greatly increased role in serious accidents. Recently, 60 percent of trucks in New York and Connecticut, and 70 percent of trucks in Maryland failed safety inspections. Sixteen states in the United States require no training at all for truck drivers.
B. There is a great deal of concern over the safety of commercial trucks since federal deregulation in 1981. Their role in serious accidents has greatly increased. Recently, 60 percent of trucks randomly stopped in Connecticut and New York and 70 percent in Maryland failed safety inspections conducted by state troopers. Sixteen states in the United States provide no training at all for truck drivers.
C. Commercial trucks have a greatly increased role in serious accidents since federal deregulation in 1981. This has led to a great deal of concern.

Recently, 70 percent of trucks in Maryland and 60 percent of trucks in New York and Connecticut failed inspection of those that were randomly stopped by state troopers. Sixteen states in the United States require no training for all truck drivers.

D. Since federal deregulation in 1981, the role that commercial trucks have played in serious accidents has greatly increased, and this has led to a great deal of concern. Recently, 60 percent of trucks in New York and Connecticut, and 70 percent of trucks in Maryland randomly stopped by state troopers failed safety inspections. Sixteen states in the U.S. don't require any training for truck drivers.

9.
I. No matter how much some people have, they still feel unsatisfied and want more, or want to keep what they have forever.
II. One recent television documentary showed several people flying from New York to Paris for a one-day shopping spree to buy platinum earrings, because they were bored.
III. In Brazil, some people were ordering coffins that cost a minimum of $45,000 and are equipping them with deluxe stereos, televisions, and other graveyard necessities.

9.____

A. Some people, despite having a great deal, still feel unsatisfied and want more, or think they can keep what they have forever. One recent documentary on television showed several people enroute from Paris to New York for a one day shopping spree to buy platinum earrings, because they were bored. Some people in Brazil are even ordering coffins equipped with such graveyard necessities as deluxe stereos and televisions. The price of the coffins start at $45,000.
B. No matter how much some people have, they may feel unsatisfied. This leads them to want more, or to want to keep what they have forever. Recently, a television documentary depicting several people flying from New York to Paris for a one day shopping spree to buy platinum earrings. They were bored. Some people in Brazil are ordering coffins that cost at least $45,000 and come equipped with deluxe televisions, stereos and other necessary graveyard items.
C. Some people will be dissatisfied no matter how much they have. They may want more, or they may want to keep what they have forever. One recent television documentary showed several people, motivated by boredom, jetting from New York to Paris for a one-day shopping spree to buy platinum earrings. In Brazil, some people are ordering coffins equipped with deluxe stereos, televisions and other graveyard necessities. The minimum price for these coffins—$45,000.
D. Some people are never satisfied. No matter how much they have they still want more, or think they can keep what they have forever. One television documentary recently showed several people flying from New York to Paris for the day to buy platinum earrings because they were bored. In Brazil, some people are ordering coffins that cost $45,000 and are equipped with deluxe stereos, televisions and other graveyard necessities.

10.
I. A television signal or video signal has three parts.
II. Its parts are the black-and-white portion, the color portion, and the synchronizing (sync) pulses, which keep the picture stable.
III. Each video source, whether it's a camera or a video-cassette recorder contains its own generator of these synchronizing pulses to accompany the picture that it's sending in order to keep it steady and straight.
IV. In order to produce a clean recording, a video-cassette recorder must "lock-up" to the sync pulses that are part of the video it is trying to record, and this effort may be very noticeable if the device does not have gunlock.

10.____

A. There are three parts to a television or video signal: the black-and-white part, the color part, and the synchronizing (sync) pulses, which keep the picture stable. Whether it's a video-cassette recorder or a camera, each video source contains its own pulse that synchronizes and generates the picture it's sending in order to keep it straight and steady. A video-cassette recorder must "lock up" to the sync pulses that are part of the video it's trying to record. If the device doesn't have gunlock, this effort must be very noticeable.

B. A video signal or television is comprised of three parts: the black-and-white portion, the color portion, and the sync (synchronizing) pulses, which keep the picture stable. Whether it's a camera or a video-cassette recorder, each video source contains its own generator of these synchronizing pulses. These accompany the picture that it's sending in order to keep it straight and steady. A video-cassette recorder must "lock up" to the sync pulses that are part of the video it is trying to record in order to produce a clean recording. This effort may be very noticeable if the device does not have gunlock.

C. There are three parts to a television or video signal: the color portion, the black-and-white portion, and the sync (synchronizing pulses). These keep the picture stable. Each video source, whether it's a video-cassette recorder or a camera, generates these synchronizing pulses accompanying the picture it's sending in order to keep it straight and steady. If a clean recording is to be produced, a video-cassette recorder must store the sync pulses that are part of the video it is trying to record. This effort may not be noticeable if the device does not have gunlock.

D. A television signal or video signal has three parts: the black-and-white portion, the color portion, and the synchronizing (sync) pulses. It's the sync pulses which keep the picture stable, which accompany it and keep it steady and straight. Whether it's a camera or a video-cassette recorder, each video source contains its own generator of these synchronizing pulses. To produce a clean recording, a video-cassette recorder must "lock up" to the sync pulses that are part of the video it is trying to record. If the device does not have gunlock, this effort may be very noticeable.

KEY (CORRECT ANSWERS)

1. C
2. B
3. A
4. B
5. D
6. A
7. B
8. D
9. C
10. D

PREPARING WRITTEN MATERIALS
EXAMINATION SECTION
TEST 1

DIRECTIONS: Each question or incomplete statement is followed by several suggested answers or completions. Select the one that BEST answers the question or completes the statement. *PRINT THE LETTER OF THE CORRECT ANSWER IN THE SPACE AT THE RIGHT.*

Questions 1-21.

DIRECTIONS: In each of the following sentences, which were taken from students' transcripts, there may be an error. Indicate the appropriate correction in the space at the right. If the sentence is correct as is, indicate this choice. Unnecessary changes will be considered incorrect.

1. In that building there seemed to be representatives of Teachers College, the Veterans Bureau, and the Businessmen's Association.
   A. Teacher's College
   B. Veterans' Bureau
   C. Businessmens Association
   D. Correct as is

   1.____

2. In his travels, he visited St. Paul, San Francisco, Springfield, Ohio, and Washington, D.C.
   A. Ohio and
   B. Saint Paul
   C. Washington, D.C.
   D. Correct as is

   2.____

3. As a result of their purchasing a controlling interest in the syndicate, it was well-known that the Bureau of Labor Statistics' calculations would be unimportant.
   A. of them purchasing
   B. well known
   C. Statistics
   D. Correct as is

   3.____

4. Walter Scott, Jr.'s, attempt to emulate his father's success was doomed to failure.
   A. Junior's,
   B. Scott's, Jr.
   C. Scott, Jr.'s attempt
   D. Correct as is

   4.____

5. About B.C. 250 the Romans invaded Great Britain, and remains of their highly developed civilization can still be seen.
   A. 250 B.C.
   B. Britain and
   C. highly-developed
   D. Correct as is

   5.____

6. The two boss's sons visited the children's department.
   A. bosses   B. bosses'   C. childrens'   D. Correct as is

   6.____

7. Miss Amex not only approved the report, but also decided that it needed no revision.
   A. report; but   B. report but   C. report. But   D. Correct as is

   7._____

8. Here's brain food in a jiffy—economical, too!
   A. economical too!   B. "brain food"
   C. jiffy-economical   D. Correct as is

   8._____

9. She said, "He likes the "Gatsby Look" very much."
   A. said "He   B. "he
   C. 'Gatsby Look'   D. Correct as is

   9._____

10. We anticipate that we will be able to visit them briefly in Los Angeles on Wednesday after a five day visit.
    A. Wednes-   B. 5 day   C. five-day   D. Correct as is

    10._____

11. She passed all her tests, and, she now has a good position.
    A. tests, and she   B. past
    C. tests;   D. Correct as is

    11._____

12. The billing clerk said, "I will send the bill today"; however, that was a week ago, and it hasn't arrived yet!
    A. today;"   B. today,"   C. ago and   D. Correct as is

    12._____

13. "She types at more-than-average speed," Miss Smith said, "but I feel that it is a result of marvelous concentration and self control on her part."
    A. more than average   B. "But
    C. self-control   D. Correct as is

    13._____

14. The state of Alaska, the largest state in the union, is also the northernmost state.
    A. Union   B. Northernmost State
    C. State of Alaska   D. Correct as is

    14._____

15. The memoirs of Ex-President Nixon, according to figures, sold more copies than Six Crises, the book he wrote in the '60s.
    A. Six Crises   B. ex-President
    C. 60s   D. Correct as is

    15._____

16. "There are three principal elements, determining the hazard of buildings: the contents hazard, the fire resistance of the structure, and the character of the interior finish," concluded the speaker.
    The one of the following statements that is MOST acceptable is that, in the above passage,
    A. the comma following the word *elements* is incorrect
    B. the colon following the word *buildings* is incorrect
    C. the comma following the word *finish* is incorrect
    D. there is no error in the punctuation of the sentence

    16._____

17. He spoke on his favorite topic, "Why We Will Win." (How could I stop him?) 17.____
    A. Win". B. him?). C. him)? C. Correct as is

18. "All any insurance policy is, is a contract for services," said my insurance 18.____
    agent, Mr. Newton.
    A. Insurance Policy B. Insurance Agent
    C. policy is is a D. Correct as is

19. Inasmuch as the price list has now been up dated, we should sent it to the 19.____
    printer.
    A. In as much B. updated
    C. pricelist D. Correct as is

20. We feel that "Our know-how" is responsible for the improvement in technical 20.____
    developments.
    A. "our B. know how C. that, D. Correct as is

21. Did Cortez conquer the Incas? the Aztecs? the South American Indians? 21.____
    A. Incas, the Aztecs, the South American Indians?
    B. Incas; the Aztecs; the South American Indians?
    C. south American Indians?
    D. Correct as is

22. Which one of the following forms for the typed name of the dictator in the closing 22.____
    lines of a letter is generally MOST acceptable in the United States?
    A. (Dr.) James F. Farley B. Dr. James F. Farley
    C. Me. James J. Farley, Ph.D. D. James F. Farley

23. The plural of 23.____
    A. turkey is turkies B. cargo is cargoes
    C. bankruptcy is bankruptcys D. son-in-law is son-in-laws

24. The abbreviation viz. means MOST NEARLY 24.____
    A. namely B. for example
    C. the following D. see

25. In the sentence, *A man in a light-gray suit waited thirty-five minutes in the* 25.____
    ante-room for the all-important document, the word IMPROPERLY hyphenated
    is
    A. light-gray B. thirty-five C. ante-room D. all-important

KEY (CORRECT ANSWERS)

1.	D		11.	A
2.	C		12.	D
3.	B		13.	D
4.	D		14.	A
5.	A		15.	B
6.	B		16.	A
7.	B		17.	D
8.	D		18.	D
9.	C		19.	B
10.	C		20.	A

21. D
22. D
23. B
24. A
25. C

TEST 2

DIRECTIONS: Each question or incomplete statement is followed by several suggested answers or completions. Select the one that BEST answers the question or completes the statement. *PRINT THE LETTER OF THE CORRECT ANSWER IN THE SPACE AT THE RIGHT.*

Questions 1-10.

DIRECTIONS: In each of the following groups of four sentences, one sentence contains an error in sentence structure, grammar, usage, diction, or punctuation. Indicate the INCORRECT sentence.

1. A. The lecture finished, the audience began asking questions.
   B. Any man who could accomplish that task the world would regard as a hero.
   C. Our respect and admiration are mutual.
   D. George did like his mother told him, despite the importunities of his playmates.

   1.____

2. A. I cannot but help admiring you for your dedication to your job.
   B. Because they had insisted upon showing us films of their travels, we have lost many friends whom we once cherished.
   C. I am constrained to admit that your remarks made me feel bad.
   D. My brother having been notified of his acceptance by the university of his choice, my father immediately made plans for a vacation.

   2.____

3. A. In no other country is freedom of speech and assembly so jealously guarded.
   B. Being a beatnik, he felt that it would be a betrayal of his cause to wear shoes and socks at the same time.
   C. Riding over the Brooklyn Bridge gave us an opportunity to see the Manhattan skyline.
   D. In 1961, flaunting SEATO, the North Vietnamese crossed the line of demarcation.

   3.____

4. A. I have enjoyed the study of the Spanish language not only because of its beauty and the opportunity it offers to understand the Hispanic culture but also to make use of it in the business associations I have in South America.
   B. The opinions he expressed were decidedly different from those he had held in his youth.
   C. Had he actually studied, he certainly would have passed.
   D. A supervisor should be patient, tactful, and firm.

   4.____

5. A. At this point we were faced with only three alternatives: to push on, to remain where we were, or to return to the village.
   B. We had no choice but to forgive so venial a sin.
   C. In their new picture, the Warners are flouting tradition.
   D. Photographs taken revealed that 2.5 square miles had been burned.

   5.____

6. A. He asked whether he might write to his friends.
    B. There are many problems which must be solved before we can be assured of world peace.
    C. Each person with whom I talked expressed his opinion freely.
    D. Holding on to my saddle with all my strength the horse galloped down the road at a terrifying pace.

7. A. After graduating high school, he obtained a position as a runner in Wall Street.
    B. Last night, in a radio address, the President urged us to subscribe to the Red Cross.
    C. In the evening, light spring rain cooled the streets.
    D. "Un-American" is a word which has been used even by those whose sympathies may well have been pro-Nazi.

8. A. It is hard to conceive of their not doing good work.
    B. Who won—you or I?
    C. He having read the speech caused much comment.
    D. Their finishing the work proves that it can be done.

9. A. Our course of study should not be different now than it was five years ago.
    B. I cannot deny myself the pleasure of publicly thanking the mayor for his actions.
    C. The article on "Morale" has appeared in the Times Literary Supplement.
    D. He died of tuberculosis contracted during service with the Allied Forces.

10. A. If it wasn't for a lucky accident, he would still be an office-clerk.
    B. It is evident that teachers need help.
    C. Rolls of postage stamps may be bought at stationery stores.
    D. Addressing machines are used by firms that publish magazines.

11. The one of the following sentences which contains NO error in usage is:
    A. After the robbers left, the proprietor stood tied in his chair for about two hours before help arrived.
    B. In the cellar I found the watchmans' hat and coat.
    C. The persons living in adjacent apartments stated that they had heard no unusual noises.
    D. Neither a knife or any firearms were found in the room.

12. The one of the following sentences which contains NO error in usage is:
    A. The policeman lay a firm hand on the suspect's shoulder.
    B. It is true that neither strength nor agility are the most important requirement for a good patrolman.
    C. Good citizens constantly strive to do more than merely comply the restraints imposed by society.
    D. Twenty years is considered a severe sentence for a felony.

13. Select the sentence containing an adverbial objective. 13._____
    A. Concepts can only acquire content when they are connected, however indirectly, with sensible experience.
    B. The cloth was several shades too light to match the skirt which she had discarded.
    C. The Gargantuan Hall of Commons became a tri-daily horror to Kurt, because two youths discerned that he had a beard and courageously told the world about it.
    D. Brooding morbidly over the event, Elsie found herself incapable of engaging in normal activity.

14. Select the sentence containing a verb in the subjunctive mood. 14._____
    A. Had he known of the new experiments with penicillin dust for the cure of colds, he might have been tempted to try them in his own office.
    B. I should be very much honored by your visit.
    C. Though he has one of the highest intelligence quotients in his group, he seems far below the average in actual achievement.
    D. Long had I known that he would be the man finally selected for such signal honors.

15. Select the sentence containing one (or more) passive perfect participle(s). 15._____
    A. Having been apprised of the consequences of his refusal to answer, the witness finally revealed the source of his information.
    B. To have been placed in such an uncomfortable position was perhaps unfair to a journalist of his reputation.
    C. When deprived of special immunity he had, of course, no alternative but to speak.
    D. Having been obdurate until now, he was reluctant to surrender under this final pressure exerted upon him.

16. Select the sentence containing a predicate nominative. 16._____
    A. His dying wish, which he expressed almost with his last breath, was to see that justice was done toward his estranged wife.
    B. So long as we continue to elect our officials in truly democratic fashion, we shall have the power to preserve our liberties.
    C. We could do nothing, at this juncture, but walk the five miles back to camp.
    D. There was the spaniel, wet and cold and miserable, waiting silently at the door.

17. Select the sentence containing exactly TWO adverbs. 17._____
    A. The gentlemen advanced with exasperating deliberateness, while his lonely partner waited.
    B. If you are well, will you come early?
    C. I think you have guessed right, though you were rather slow, I must say.
    D. The last hundred years have seen more change than a thousand years of the Roman Empire, than a hundred thousand years of the stone age.

Questions 18-24.

DIRECTIONS: Select the choice describing the error in the sentence.

18. If us seniors do not support school functions, who will?
    A. Unnecessary shift in tense
    B. Incomplete sentence
    C. Improper case of pronoun
    D. Lack of parallelism

19. The principal has issued regulations which, in my opinion, I think are too harsh.
    A. Incorrect punctuation
    B. Faulty sentence structure
    C. Misspelling
    D. Redundant expression

20. The freshmens' and sophomores' performances equaled those of the juniors and seniors.
    A. Ambiguous reference
    B. Incorrect placement of punctuation
    C. Misspelling of past tense
    D. Incomplete comparison

21. Each of them, Anne and her, is an outstanding pianist I can't tell you which one is best.
    A. Lack of agreement
    B. Improper degree of comparison
    C. Incorrect case of pronoun
    D. Run-on sentence

22. She wears clothes that are more expensive than my other friends.
    A. Misuse of *than*
    B. Incorrect relative pronoun
    C. Shift in tense
    D. Faulty comparison

23. At the very end of the story it implies that the children's father died tragically.
    A. Misuse of *implies*
    B. Indefinite use of pronoun
    C. Incorrect spelling
    D. Incorrect possessive

24. At the end of the game both of us, John and me, couldn't scarcely walk because we were so tired.
    A. Incorrect punctuation
    B. Run-on sentence
    C. Incorrect case of pronoun
    D. Double negative

Questions 25-30.

DIRECTIONS: Questions 25 through 30 consist of a sentence lacking certain needed punctuation. Pick as your answer the description of punctuation which will CORRECTLY complete the sentence.

25. If you take the time to keep up your daily correspondence you will no doubt be most efficient.
    A. Comma only after *doubt*
    B. Comma only after *correspondence*
    C. Commas after *correspondence*, *will*, and *be*
    D. Commas after *if*, *correspondence*, and *will*

26. Because he did not send the application soon enough he did not receive the   26.____
    up to date copy of the book.
    A. Commas after *application* and *enough,* and quotation marks before *up* and after *date*
    B. Commas after *application* and *enough,* and hyphens between *to* and *date*
    C. Comma after *enough,* and hyphens between *up* and *to* and between *to* and *date*
    D. Comma after *application,* and quotation marks before *up* and after *date*

27. The coordinator requested from the department the following items a letter each   27.____
    week summarizing progress personal forms and completed applications for tests.
    A. Commas after *items* and *completed*
    B. Semi-colon after *items* and *progress,* comma after *forms*
    C. Colon after *items,* commas after *progress* and *forms*
    D. Colon after *items,* commas after *forms* and *applications*

28. The supervisor asked Who will attend the conference next month.   28.____
    A. Comma after *asked,* period after *month*
    B. Period after *asked,* question mark after *month*
    C. Comma after *asked,* quotation marks before *Who,* quotation marks after *month,* and question mark after the quotation marks
    D. Comma after *asked,* quotation marks before *Who,* question mark after *month,* and quotation marks after the question mark

29. When the statistics are collected, we will forward the results to you as soon as   29.____
    possible.
    A. Comma after *you*
    B. Commas after *forward* and *you*
    C. Commas after *collected, results* and *you*
    D. Comma after *collected*

30. The ecology of our environment is concerned with mans pollution of the   30.____
    atmosphere.
    A. Comma after *ecology*
    B. Apostrophe after *n* and before *s* in *mans*
    C. Commas after *ecology* and *environment*
    D. Apostrophe after *s* in *mans*

KEY (CORRECT ANSWERS)

1.	D	11.	C	21.	B
2.	A	12.	D	22.	D
3.	D	13.	B	23.	B
4.	A	14.	A	24.	D
5.	B	15.	A	25.	B
6.	D	16.	A	26.	C
7.	A	17.	C	27.	C
8.	C	18.	C	28.	D
9.	A	19.	D	29.	D
10.	A	20.	B	30.	B

TEST 3

DIRECTIONS: Each question or incomplete statement is followed by several suggested answers or completions. Select the one that BEST answers the question or completes the statement. *PRINT THE LETTER OF THE CORRECT ANSWER IN THE SPACE AT THE RIGHT.*

Questions 1-6.

DIRECTIONS: From the four choices offered in Questions 1 through 6, select the one which is INCORRECT.

1. A. Before we try to extricate ourselves from this struggle in which we are now engaged in, we must be sure that we are not severing ties of honor and duty.
   B. Besides being an outstanding student, he is also a leader in school government and a trophy-winner in school sports.
   C. If the framers of the Constitution were to return to life for a day, their opinion of our amendments would be interesting.
   D. Since there are three m's in the word, it is frequently misspelled.

1.____

2. A. It was a college with an excellance beyond question.
   B. The coach will accompany the winners, whomever they may be.
   C. The dean, together with some other faculty members, is planning a conference.
   D. The jury are arguing among themselves.

2.____

3. A. This box is less nearly square than that one.
   B. Wagner is many persons' choice as the world's greatest composer.
   C. The habits of Copperheads are different from Diamond Backs.
   D. The teacher maintains that the child was insolent.

3.____

4. A. There was a time when the Far North was unknown territory. Now American soldiers manning radar stations there wave to Boeing jet planes zooming by overhead.
   B. Exodus, the psalms, and Deuteronomy are all books of the Old Testament.
   C. Linda identified her china dishes by marking their bottoms with india ink.
   D. Harry S. Truman, former president of the United States, served as a captain in the American army during World War I.

4.____

5. A. The sequel of their marriage was a divorce.
   B. We bought our car secondhand.
   C. His whereabouts is unknown.
   D. Jones offered to use his own car, providing the company would pay for gasoline, oil, and repairs,

5.____

6. A. I read Golding's "Lord of the Flies". 6.____
   B. The orator at the civil rights rally thrilled the audience when he said, "I quote Robert Burns's line, 'A man's a man for a' that."
   C. The phrase "producer to consumer" is commonly used by market analysts.
   D. The lawyer shouted, "Is not this evidence illegal?"

Questions 7-9.

DIRECTIONS: In answering Questions 7 through 9, mark the letter A if faulty because of incorrect grammar, mark the letter B if faulty because of incorrect punctuation, mark the letter C if correct.

7. Mr. Brown our accountant, will audit the accounts next week. 7.____

8. Give the assignment to whomever is able to do it most efficiently. 8.____

9. The supervisor expected either your or I to file these reports. 9.____

Questions 10-14.

DIRECTIONS: In each of the following groups of four sentences, one sentence contains an error in sentence structure, grammar, usage, diction, or punctuation. Indicate the INCORRECT sentence.

10. A. The agent asked, "Did you say, 'Never again?'" 10.____
    B. Kindly let me know whether you can visit us on the 17th.
    C. "I cannot accept that!" he exploded. "Please show me something else.
    D. Ed, will you please lend me your grass shears for an hour or so.

11. A. Recalcitrant though he may have been, Alexander was willfully destructive. 11.____
    B. Everybody should look out for himself.
    C. John is one of those students who usually spends most of his time in the principal's office.
    D. She seems to feel that what is theirs is hers.

12. A. Be he ever so much in the wrong, I'll support the man while deploring his actions. 12.____
    B. The schools' lack of interest in consumer education is shortsighted.
    C. I think that Fitzgerald's finest stanza is one which includes the reference to youth's "sweet-scented manuscript.
    D. I never would agree to Anderson having full control of the company's policies.

13. A. We had to walk about five miles before finding a gas station. 13.____
    B. The willful sending of a false alarm has, and may, result in homicide.
    C. Please bring that book to me at once.
    D. Neither my sister nor I am interested in bowling.

14. A. He is one of the very few football players who doesn't wear a helmet with a face guard.
    B. But three volunteers appeared at the recruiting office.
    C. Such consideration as you can give us will be appreciated.
    D. When I left them, the group were disagreeing about the proposed legislation.

14.____

Question 15.

DIRECTIONS: Question 15 contains two sentences concerning criminal law. The sentences could contain errors in English grammar or usage. A sentence does not contain an error simply because it could be written in a different manner. In answering this question, choose answer
A. if only sentence I is correct
B. if only sentence II is correct
C. if both sentences are correct
D. if neither sentence is correct

15. I. The use of fire or explosives to destroy tangible property is proscribed by the criminal mischief provisions of the Revised Penal Law.
    II. The defendant's taking of a taxicab for the immediate purpose of affecting his escape did not constitute grand larceny.

15.____

KEY (CORRECT ANSWERS)

1.	A	6.	A	11.	C
2.	B	7.	B	12.	D
3.	C	8.	A	13.	B
4.	B	9.	A	14.	A
5.	D	10	A	15.	A

MENTAL DISORDERS AND TREATMENT PRACTICES

This section reviews eight areas that are usually tested on examinations:

- The Characteristics of Various Psychiatric Disorders
- The Needs of Special Groups (Children, Geriatrics)
- The Influences of Environment, Society, and Family on Psychiatric Disorders
- Psychotropic Drugs (Reactions and Uses)
- The Assessment and Evaluation of Patients
- The Functions and Purposes of the Treatment Team
- The Development and Implementation of the Treatment Plan
- Methods for Handling People with Various Emotional or Psychiatric Disorders

THE CHARACTERISTICS OF VARIOUS PSYCHIATRIC DISORDERS

It is often difficult to assign labels to human behavior with any large degree of accuracy. Behavior sometimes changes rapidly, and the interpretation of what behavior a label actually represents can vary greatly from one person to the next. One can often learn a great deal more about a person by observing their behavior than by reading a diagnostic label about that person. Regardless, diagnostic labels can be helpful to members of a treatment team as a shorthand method of describing a group of behaviors one might expect from certain individuals. They are also required for many insurance forms. A diagnosis may be useful as long as one views the diagnosis as an ongoing process, and can continue to look at the patient with *new eyes*.

The Difference Between Neurosis and Psychosis

People suffering from a neurosis are usually able to manage with the concerns of daily life, although there is often some distortion in their concept of reality. Those suffering from a neurosis may feel inferior, unloved, or have a long-term feeling of fear or dread. They may have obsessions, compulsions or phobias, but they are rarely dangerous to themselves or others. They usually have some insight into their problems, and except in severe cases, don't require hospitalization. Many go through life without obtaining any help for their problems. Those who experience a psychosis, however, are out of touch with reality and live in an imaginary world. They may hear voices, feel that they are being persecuted, or experience very deep depressions. There is a very definite split between the reality of those suffering from psychoses and the reality of the world. Unlike those suffering from neuroses, those suffering from psychoses often lose track of time, person, and place, and they have little insight into the nature of their behavior. They usually require hospitalization and their behavior is sometimes injurious to other people or themselves, although they may insist that there is nothing wrong with them.

Categories of Neurosis

It is important to keep in mind that rarely will all of a patient's symptoms fall into any one category, and that symptoms may change over time from one category to another. *Anxiety Neuroses* constitute approximately 35% of all neurotic disorders. Those suffering from anxiety neuroses have a tendency to view the world as hostile and cruel, and may frequently restrict daily activities in order to feel safer in their environment. They often feel tense, worried, and anxious, but are unable to articulate exactly why they feel this way. Many anxious individuals are very uncertain of themselves in even minor stress producing situations, and they may have real difficulties in concentrating because of their high anxiety levels.

Other symptoms may include strong anxiety reactions with difficulty catching one's breath, perspiration, increased heart beat, dizziness, and feeling that they are dying. They may come to the Emergency Room of a hospital complaining of a heart attack or heart troubles. It is important to keep in mind that many elements of the anxiety reaction are seen in patients with other neurotic disorders.

Conversion Reactions or *Hysteria* involve the loss of ability to perform some physical function that the person could previously perform, which is psychogenic in origin. This reaction is an attempt by the individual to defend herself or himself from some anxiety producing situation by developing physical symptoms that have no organic or physical cause. These reactions are not common, and constitute less than five percent of neurotic disorders. The lost function is often symbolically related to a situation which has produced stress or anxiety, and is often an attempt to escape from that situation. The person may lose the ability to hear or speak, have unusual bodily sensations, or lose control of some motor function. Since there is no physical cause of dysfunction, some people assume that the pain or paralysis is not real, or that this type of person is faking. *Dissociative Reactions* also serve to protect the individual from particularly stressful situations. Amnesia, fugue, and multiple personalities are the major categories of dissociative reactions. Despite the prevalence of *amnesia* on soap operas, dissociative reactions account for less than five percent of all neurotic disorders. Amnesiacs usually forget specific information for a specified but variable period of time. The patient does not, however, forget his or her basic lifestyle or habits. In *fugue*, the person combines the amnesia with flight, and leaves the area where the stressful situation is. Usually the person is unaware of where he or she has been, or where he or she is going. There are very few cases of *multiple personalities*. In this disorder, the person shows different ways of responding to the environment. Each individual personality within the person is a complete personality system, and may dominate the person's reactions to his or her environment, depending upon the situation.

Obsessive-Compulsive Reactions involve either the inability to stop thinking about something the person does not want to think about, or the obligatory performance of a repetitive act. People experiencing these reactions often recognize they are irrational, but are unable to stop doing them. They often attempt to rearrange their environment, which they may perceive as threatening, in an attempt to impose control and structure, so they can control their environment and feel safer. Those suffering from compulsive reactions feel a strong need to perform or repeat certain behaviors, often in order to prevent something terrible from happening to them. (This might involve pre-determined ways to enter a room, brush their teeth, get into bed, begin conversations, etc.) Of course, many people may exhibit aspects of this behavior. Observing some professional baseball players before they pitch or take a pitch can certainly demonstrate this point. There is little cause for concern if the patterns are relatively temporary and help the person in some way obtain their goal. When the behaviors begin to unduly restrict a person's activities, then the situation becomes more serious. People exhibiting this behavior are often unable to make decisions effectively, are often perfectionists, have a strong need for structure, and are fairly rigid. Those who are obsessed with unwanted thoughts may have quite a variety of areas that they think about. The most common areas, however, concern religion, ethical concerns (something being absolutely right or wrong), bodily functions, and suicide.

Phobic Reactions involve a strong, persistent irrational fear of an object, condition, or place. It is believed that phobias usually involve a displacement of anxiety from the original cause to the phobic object. The phobia serves to assist the individual in avoiding the anxiety-causing situation. Some of the most common phobias include fear of crowds, being alone, darkness, thunderstorms, and high places. It is often very difficult to discover the symbolic significance of a particular phobia.

Neurotic Depressive Reactions involve an intensification of normal grief reactions. Research has indicated that those suffering from this reaction are unable to *bounce back* from upsetting or discouraging events. People who suffer from this reaction tend to have a poor self-concept, exaggerated dependency needs, a tendency to feel guilty about almost anything, and to turn those guilt feelings against themselves in a highly punitive way. The possibility of suicide should be kept in mind when working with these patients.

Categories of Psychosis

Psychoses are generally divided into two categories, *functional psychoses* and *organic psychoses*. Functional psychoses are caused by psychological stress, while organic psychoses are caused by a disorder of the brain for which physical pathology can be demonstrated. A third category, *toxic psychoses,* is sometimes used to refer to psychotic reactions caused by toxic substances such as drugs or poisons.

Schizophrenia accounts for approximately 25 percent of all first admissions to mental institutions, and is the largest single diagnostic group of psychotic patients. The *paranoid schizophrenic* shows a great deal of suspiciousness and hostility, and may be very aggressive. The *simple type schizophrenic* is shy and withdrawn, and shows interest in his or her environment. The *hebephrenic schizophrenic* often has bizarre mannerisms and may appear quite manic. He or she may laugh and giggle inappropriately, and become preoccupied with unimportant matters. The *catatonic schizophrenic* may remain motionless for days or hours, and may refuse to eat. The two phases of catatonia are the *stuporous phase* where the person is motionless and *catatonic excitement* where the person is over-active and appears manic. While the catatonic schizophrenic may alternate between these two phases, most show a preference for just one. Someone suffering from *schizoaffective schizophrenia* will have significant thought disorders and mood variations. They may initially appear to be depressed or manic, but a basic personality disorganization also exists. These are the major categories of schizophrenia you should need for the exam. Since the exam announcement states basic knowledge is required, it is very possible some of the above categories may be too specific. We have included them just in case, however.

The general symptoms of schizophrenia include an inability to deal with reality, the presence of hallucinations or delusions, inappropriate emotions, autism and various other unusual behaviors. There is often a very noticeable inability to organize thoughts. Schizophrenic reactions that occur suddenly are referred to as *acute* schizophrenic reactions, while those that develop slowly over a rather lengthy period are called *chronic* schizophrenic reactions.

Paranoid Reactions in people account for less than one percent of psychiatric admissions. Those with this behavior usually mistrust the motives of everyone, are very resentful, and often hostile. They may show signs of grandiosity or persecution. The person often believes that whatever happens is related to him or her. The major difference between paranoid patients and paranoid schizophrenics is that the paranoid patient usually has better control of his or her thought processes, and is able to make more appropriate responses to situations. They are usually more reality-oriented, and able to state their feelings more effectively.

Affective Reactions are those that represent a change in the normal affect, or mood, of a person. There are two major categories of affective disorders: *manic-depressive reactions* and *involutional psychotic reactions*. In the manic-depressive reaction, the manic and depressive states alternate. In the manic phase, the person may be extremely talkative, agitated or elated, and demonstrate a great deal of physical and verbal activity. They may also exhibit some grandiosity. In the depressive phase, the person is joyless, quiet, and inhibited. The manic reactions are often divided into three degress of severity, each category representing a more severe degree of manic reaction. *Hypomania* is the least severe, *acute mania* is the next, and *delirious mania* is the most severe state. The term *involutional psychosis is* usually related to a patient's age. For women, the involutional age is considered to be somewhere between 40 and 55, and the involutional period for men is somewhere between 50 and 65. It seems that stresses are greater for men and women during these periods, and that these stresses may trigger psychotic reactions which are generally transient. These people generally have a long history of feeling guilty and very anxious, have little diversity of activity, and few sources of satisfaction in their lives.

Selected Personality Disorders

This category includes behavior which is maladaptive, but neither psychotic nor neurotic. This group includes *antisocial reactions,* the *abuse of alchol and other drugs,* and *sexual deviations*. The *antisocial* or *sociopathic* personality type fails to develop a concern for others and uses relationships to get what he or she wants. There is little or no concern about what effect their behavior might have on others, and they seldom feel remorse or guilt. They are often likable, friendly, intelligent people. Their relationships with others tend to be superficial, however, because they lack the capacity for deep emotional responses. The sociopath is often impulsive and seeks immediate gratification of his or her wants. He or she often is unreliable, untruthful, undependable and insincere. A large number of people have sociopathic traits which, as with most other characteristics, vary in severity and number. Sociopaths are found in all professions, although many are able to control their acting out behaviors or channel them in more socially acceptable ways. They avoid acting out not because of internal values, but because they do not wish to get caught. Sociopaths usually have a low frustration tolerance, are easily bored, and continually seek excitement. The sociopath most frequently comes to treatment because he or she has been *caught* doing something or been required to seek help by an employer or family member.

Sexual Deviations occur in those who fail to develop what their society considers appropriate sexual behavior. The major sexual deviations include child molestation, rape, sadism, masochism, voyeurism, fetishism, transvestism, exhibitionism, pedophilia, and incest. As you can see, some of these behaviors are much more harmful to other people than others are.

PSYCHOTROPIC DRUGS (REACTIONS AND USES)

The two major classifications of the psychotropic drugs are the tranquilizers, which are further divided into major (or anti-psychotic) and minor (or antianxiety) groups, and the antidepressants. Other drugs used include anticonvulsants, sedatives, hypnotics, and antiparkinsons.

Tranquilizers are meant to calm disturbed patients, and free them from agitation or disturbance. Drugs designed as *antipsychotic,* or *major tranquilizers,* also help to reduce the frequency of hallucinations, delusions, thought disorders, and the type of withdrawal seen in catatonic schizophrenia. It may take several days of drug therapy before the symptoms begin to subside, but during this time the patient becomes less fearful, hostile and upset by his disturbed sensory perceptions. The *phenothiazine derivatives* are the largest group of antipsychotic drugs. All the drugs in this group have essentially the same type of action on the body, but vary according to strength and the type and severity of their side effects. These drugs include:

Thorazine	Trilafon	Taractan
Mellaril	Compazine	Navane
Stelazine	Dartal	Sordinal
Prolixin	Proketazine	Haldol
Sparine	Tindal	Loxitane
Vesprin	Repoise	Moban

Serious side effects are very important to watch for. For these drugs, the phenothiazine derivatives, there are three major types of extrapyramidal symptoms (EPS): (1) akinesia - inability to sit still, complaints of fatigue and weakness, and continuous movement of the hands, mouth, and body; (2) pseudoparkinsonism - restlessness, mask-like facial expressions, drooling, and tremors; (3) tardive dyskenesia - lack of control over voluntary movements. Symptoms may include involuntary grimacing, sucking and chewing movements, pursing of the tongue and mouth, jerking of the hands, feet and neck, and drooping head. Immediate action must be taken to combat these side effects. The administration of antiparkinson drugs usually produces a dramatic reduction in symptoms. Unless spotted and treated early, however, these can become permanent.

Other side effects may include muscle spasms, shuffling gait, skin rash, eye problems, trembling hands and fingers, fainting, wormlike tongue movements, sore throat and fever, yellowing of skin or eyes, dry mouth, constipation, excessive weight gain, edema, a drop in blood pressure when moving from a lying to standing position, decreased sexual interest, sensitivity to light and prone to sunburn and visual problems, blurred vision, drowsiness, and increased perspiration. Just about any physical symptom or behavior could be caused by a reaction to a drug.

Special Considerations: Patients receiving a high dose of a phenothiazine drug should have their blood pressure checked regularly. Long exposures of skin to sunlight should be avoided (a wide-brimmed hat and long-sleeved clothing can also help). If a patient receiving phenothiazines is lethargic and wants to sleep a great deal, the dose of the drug may be too high and need adjustment. Patients on phenothiazines should not drive or use dangerous equipment. These drugs greatly increase the effects of alcohol. In the first three to five days, a person may feel drowsy and dizzy upon standing. Antipsychotic drugs tend to mask the symptoms of diseases and dictate that patients receiving them undergo thorough physical examinations every six months.

The *Minor Tranquilizers*, or *antianxiety drugs*, reduce anxiety and muscle tension associated with it. They are useful primarily with psychoneurotic and psychosomatic disorders. When given in small doses, they are relatively safe and have few side effects. Unlike the antipsychotic drugs, some of the antianxiety drugs tend to be habit-forming. If the drug is discontinued, the person may experience severe withdrawal symptoms, such as convulsions or delirium. These drugs include:

Librium	Milpath	Frienquel
Azene	Deprol	Phobex
Tranxene	Milprem	Softran
Valium	Miltown	Atarax
Ativan	Robaxin	Vistaril
Serax	Solacen	Trancopal

Side effects may include rashes, chills, fever, nausea, headaches, poor muscle coordination, some inability to concentrate, and dizziness. Excessive amounts of these drugs may lead to coma and death; however, death is less likely with an overdose of minor tranquilizers than with an overdose of barbituates. Patients taking these should be cautioned against driving or performing tasks that require careful attention to detail and mental alertness.

Antidepressants, such as the *Tricyclic Antidepressants,* are used to elevate the patient's mood, and increase appetite and mental and physical alertness. Drugs in this group tend to take one to four weeks of use before significant changes occur in the patient's outlook. Since these drugs sometimes excite patients instead of sedating them, patients must be observed closely for reactions. These drugs include:

Elavil	Sinequan
Endep	Tofranil
Asendine	Aventyl
Morpramin	Vivactil
Adapin	Marplan
Presamine	Janimine

Common side effects include dry mouth, fatigue, weakness, nausea, increased appetite, increased perspiration, heartburn, and sensitivity to sunlight. *Serious side effects* include blurred vision, constipation, irregular heartbeat, problems urinating, headache, eye pain, fainting, hallucination, vomiting, unusually slow pulse, seizures, skin rash, sore throat and fever, and yellowing of eyes and skin.

Serious side effects include blurred vision, constipation, irregular heartbeat, problems urinating, headache, eye pain, fainting, hallucination, vomiting, unusually slow pulse, seizures, skin rash, sore throat and fever, and yellowing of eyes and skin.

Monoamineoxidose Inhibitors (MAO Inhibitors) are sometimes used for depression, but can have *very* serious side effects, and can also lead to serious hypertensive crisis. Their use must be very closely monitored. Their use with some over-the-counter drugs can be very serious. Foods containing Typtophen or Tyramine (some examples: caffeine, chocolate, herring, beans, chicken liver, cheese, beer, pickles, wine) should be avoided also. *Side effects* to watch for include severe headaches, stiff neck, nausea, vomiting, dilated pupils, and cold, clammy skin. A hypertensive crisis requires *immediate* treatment. These drugs include: Marplan, Nardil, Parnate, and Ludiomil.

In addition to the above psychotropic drugs, sedatives, hypnotics, anticonvulsants, and antiparkinsons drugs are also used. Since the exam announcement includes uses and reactions of only the psychotropic drugs, we will not review the non-psychotropic drugs. We will mention, however, the use and reactions of *Lithium Carbonate* (also known as Eskolith, Lithane,

Lithobid, and Lithonate). This drug is primarily used in the treatment of manic depressive psychoses since it is effective in decreasing excessive motor activity, talking, and unstable behavior by acting on the brain's metabolism. It also decreases swings in mood. The correct dose is close to the overdose level for this drug, so it is important to watch closely for symptoms and to report them immediately. *Common side effects* include dry mouth, metal taste, slightly increased urination, hand tremors, increased appetite, and fatigue. *Serious side effects* include greatly increased urination, nausea, vomiting, diarrhea, loss of muscle coordination, muscle cramps or weakness, irritability, confusion, slurred speech, blackout spells, and coma. These side effects require medical attention. *Special Considerations:* This drug must sometimes be taken from one to several weeks before the resident feels better. Hot weather, hot baths, and too much exercise can be dangerous, as too much perspiring can lead to an overdose. The person should drink two to three quarts of fluid a day, but should not drink large quantities of caffeine-containing beverages like coffee, tea, or colas.

GLOSSARY OF BASIC PSYCHIATRIC TERMS

TABLE OF CONTENTS

	Page
Accident Prone ... Anxiety	1
Anxiety Reaction (Anxiety Neurosis) ... Catatonic State	2
Character Disorder ... Conversion	3
Conversion Reaction ... Depression	4
Disorientation ... Environment	5
Epilepsy ... Free Association	6
Frustration ... Hypnosis (Hypnotic Trance)	7
Hypochondriasis ... Insight	8
Instinct ... Looseness of Association	9
Maladjustment ... Mind	10
Motivation ... Object	11
Obsession ... Paranoid State	12
Pathogenesis ... Projective Tests	13
Psyche ... Psychosomatic	14
Psychosurgery ... Reversal	15
Sadism ... Stress	16
Subject ... Turning Against the Self	17
Unconscious ... Waxy Flexibility	18

GLOSSARY OF BASIC PSYCHIATRIC TERMS

A

ACCIDENT PRONE
Special susceptibility to accidents due to psychological causes.
ADDICTION
A descriptive name for a type of psychiatric illness (character disorder) characterized by excessive psychological and/or physiologic dependence upon the intake of some substance, as, for example, alcohol or an opiate.
ADJUSTMENT
The series of technics or processes by which the individual strives to meet the continuous changes that take place within himself and in his environment. Synonym: adaptation. (Some authorities consider adjustment to refer particularly to psychological activity and adaptation to physiologic activity.)
AFFECT
Generalized feeling tone. (Usually considered to be more persistent than emotion and less so than mood.)
Affective, pertaining to affect.
Affective psychosis, a psychosis characterized by an extreme alteration in mood in the direction of mania or of depression.
AGGRESSION (Aggressive Drive)
A term used in various ways; in the usq.ge of psychiatry, an instinct-like force, much influenced by early experience, motivating the individual to destructive activity.
AIM
Intention or purpose; in psychiatric literature the term is used chiefly in the discussion of instincts; the *aim* of an instinctual drive may be defined as an action on the part of the individual that involves the *object* of the drive and results in gratification. Thus, the aim of the instinctual drive, hunger, is eating.
AMBIVALENCE
The experiencing of contradictory strivings or emotions toward an object or situation. In extreme form, characteristic of *schizophrenia.*
ANAL CHARACTER (PERSONALITY)
(1) In psychoanalysis a pattern of behavior in an adult that originates in the anal eroticism of infancy and is characterized by such traits as excessive orderliness, miserliness, and obstinacy.
(2) A type of character (personality) disorder in which many of the individual's conflicts and defenses remain those appropriate to the muscle-training period, usually characterized by such traits as parsimony, rigidity, and pedantry.
ANAL PERIOD
One of the developmental stages; the muscle-training period.
ANTHROPOLOGY
The science of man or mankind in the widest sense; the history of human society; the developmental aspects of man as a species.
ANXIETY
(1) Apprehension, the source of which is largely unknown or unrecognized. It is different from fear, which is the emotional response to a consciously recognized and usually external danger.
(2) A state of tension and distress akin to fear, but produced by the threatened loss of inner control rather than by an external danger.

Anxiety attack, a phenomenon characterized by intense feelings of anxiety plus such physiologic manifestations as increased pulse and respiratory rates and increased perspiration.

ANXIETY REACTION (ANXIETY NEUROSIS)

A *psychoneurosis* characterized by the more or less continuous presence of anxiety in excess of normal and occasional clear-cut *anxiety attacks*.

ATTITUDE

One's physical and emotional position and manner with respect to another person, thing, or situation.

Attitude therapy, a method of treatment utilizing the assumption by the personnel of attitudes calculated to exert a favorable effect upon the patient.

AUTISM

Self-preoccupation with loss of interest in and appreciation of other persons and socially accepted behavior. *Autistic thinking,* thought processes determined by inner needs and relatively uninfluenced by environmental considerations, a characteristic of *schizophrenia*.

AUTISTIC CHILD

In child psychiatry, a child who responds chiefly to inner thoughts who does not relate to his environment, and whose overall functioning is immature and often appears retarded.

B

BASIC DRIVE

In human psychology, one of a group of hereditarily transmitted motivating forces, deriving ultimately from biochemical changes within the organism; used synonymously with instinct.

BEHAVIOR (HUMAN)

All the activity of a human being that is capable of observation by another person.

BEHAVIOR DISORDER

See Personality Disorder.

BLOCKING

(1) Difficulty in recollection, or interruption of a train of thought or speech, caused by unconscious emotional factors.
(2) An involuntary, functional interference with a person's thinking, memory or communication. (Usually the term is employed with reference to a psychotherapeutic situation.)

C

CASTRATION

Literally, the removal or the destruction of the gonads (ovaries or testes). In psychoanalytic terminology, the loss of the penis.

CASTRATION ANXIETY

Anxiety due to danger (fantasied) of loss of the genitals or injuries to them. May be precipitated by everyday events that have symbolic significance and appear to be threatening, such as loss of job, loss of a tooth, or an experience of ricidule or humiliation.

CATALEPSY

A condition usually characterized by trance-like states. May occur in organic or psychological disorders or under hypnosis.

CATATONIC STATE (Catatonia)

(1) A state characterized by immobility with, muscular rigidity or inflexibility and at times by excitability. Virtually always a symptom of schizophrenia.
(2) One of the four classic schizophrenic subgroups (syndromes), usually beginning at a

relatively early age and characterized by a rapid onset and interference with normal motor function.

CHARACTER DISORDER
See Personality Disorder.

COMPENSATION
(1) A defense mechanism, operating unconsciously, by which the individual attempts to make up for (i.e., to compensate for) real or fancied deficiencies.
(2) A conscious process in which the individual strives to make up for real or imagined defects in such areas as physique, performance, skills, or psychological attributes.

COMPLEX
(1) A group of associated ideas that have a common emotional tie. These are largely unconscious and significantly influence attitudes and associations. Examples are:

Inferiority Complex - Feelings of inferiority stemming from real or imagined physical or social inadequacies that may cause anxiety or other adverse reactions. The individual may overcompensate by excessive ambition or by the development of special skills, often in the very field in which he was originally handicapped.

Oedipus Complex - Attachment of the child for the parent of the opposite sex, accompanied by envious and aggressive feelings toward the parent of the same sex. These feelings are largely repressed (i.e., made unconscious) because of the fear of displeasure or punishment by the parent of the same sex. In its original use, the term applied only to the male child.

(2) In psychoanalytic terminology, a group of associated ideas and feelings that, though unconscious, influence the subject's conscious attitudes and behavior.

COMPULSION
(1) An insistent, repetitive, and unwanted urge to perform an act that is contrary to the person's ordinary conscious wishes or standards. Failure to perform the compulsive act results in overt anxiety.
(2) An act that is carried out, in some degree, against the subject's conscious wishes, either to avoid the anxiety that would otherwise appear, or to dispel a disturbing *obsession*.
compulsive, pertaining to a compulsion.

COMPULSIVE PERSONALITY
A type of personality disorder; more specifically, a type of neurotic personality. *See* Anal Character (Personality).

CONFLICT
A struggle between two or more opposing forces. *Intrapersonal (intrapsychic; conflict,* a struggle between forces within a single personality. *Interpersonal conflict,* a struggle between two or more individuals.

CONGENITAL
Present from birth; mayor may not be hereditary.

CONSCIENCE
Equivalent to the conscious portion of the superego; in strict psychoanalytic terminology, the "ego ideal."

CONSCIOUS
Aware or sensible; "mentally awake."

CONVERSION
Sensory or motor dysfunctions by which the subject gives symbolic expression to a conflict (of which he is not conscious).

CONVERSION REACTION

A psychoneurosis, formerly called "conversion hysteria," characterized by conversions.

CULTURE

The characteristic attainments of a people.

CYCLOTHYMIA

A tendency or a proneness to repeated, exaggerated, largely irrational alterations in mood, usually between euphoria and depression.

Cyclothymic, pertaining to cyclothymia.

Cyclothymia personality, a type of psychotic personality disorder, often the precursor of manic-depressive psychosis.

D

DEATH INSTINCT (Thanatos)

In Freudian theory, the unconscious drive toward dissolution and death. Coexists with and is in opposition to the life instinct (Eros).

DEFENSE MECHANISM

(1) A specific process, operating unconsciously, that is employed to seek relief from emotional conflict and freedom from anxiety.

(2) A psychological technic performed by the ego but carried out below the subject's threshold of awareness, designed to ward off anxiety or unpleasant tensions.

DELIRIUM

An altered level of consciousness (awareness), often acute and in most instances reversible, manifested by disorientation and confusion and induced by an interference with the metabolic processes of the neurons of the brain. *Delirium tremens,* an agitated delirious state occurring as a complication of chronic alcoholism.

DELUSION

A fixed idea, arising out of the subject's inner needs and contrary to the observed facts as these are interpreted by normal persons under the same circumstances; a symptom of psychosis.

DEMENTIA

A chronic, typically irreversible deterioration of intellectual capacities, due to organic disease of the brain that has produced structural changes (the actual death of neurons).

Dementia paralytica, formerly "paresis," a chronic syphilitic inflammation of the brain and its membranous coverings resulting, if untreated, in progressive dementia and paralysis and ultimately in death.

Dementia praecox, an old (obsolescent) (and misleading) term for schizophrenia.

DENIAL

A *defense mechanism* in which the ego refuses to allow awareness of some aspect of reality.

DEPRESSION

(1) Psychiatrically, a morbid sadness, dejection, or melancholy; to be differentiated from grief, which is realistic and proportionate to what has been lost. A depression may be a symptom of any psychiatric disorder or may constitute its principal manifestation.

(2) A pathologic state brought on by feelings of loss and/or guilt and characterized by sadness and a lowering of self-esteem.

Neurotic depressive reaction, a state of depression of neurotic intensity in which *reality-testing* is largely unimpaired and in which physiologic disturbances, if present, are usually mild.

Psychotic depressive reaction, a state of depression of psychotic intensity in which reality-testing is severely impaired and in which physiologic disturbances *(vegetative signs)* are usually conspicuous.

Reactive depression, a state of depression -- intensity not specified -- for which the precipitating stress can be clearly discerned and seen to be of some magnitude.

DISORIENTATION

Confusion of the subject with respect to such information as the correct time and place, a knowledge of his personal identity and an understanding of his situation; typically seen in *delirium* and *dementia.*

DISPLACEMENT

A general term for a group of psychological phenomena (technics) in which certain strivings or feelings are (unconsciously) transferred from one object, activity, or situation to another (which acquires a similar meaning). The defense technic of sublimation is one example of a successful displacement.

DISSOCIATION

A breaking of psychic connections, of associations.

DISSOCIATIVE REACTION

Formerly called "hysterical amnesia." A psychoneurosis in which a group of thoughts, feelings and memories becomes separated from the rest of the personality.

DRIVE

See Basic Drive.

DYNAMIC (PSYCHODYNAMIC)

Pertaining to the forces operating within the personality and determining the behavior, particularly unconscious forces. Dynamic psychiatry, a psychiatry concerned with the understanding of such motivating forces.

E

EGO

(1) In psychoanalytic theory, one of the three major divisions of human personality, the others being the id and superego. The ego, commonly identified with consciousness of self, is the mental agent mediating among three contending forces: the external demands of social pressure or reality; the primitive instinctual demands arising from the id imbedded as it is in the deepest level of the unconscious; and the claims of the superego, born of parental and social prohibitions and functioning as an internal censor or "conscience."

(2) One of the three agencies or aspects of the mind, the ego is the aspect that is in contact with the environment through the sensory apparatus, that appriases environmental and inner changes and that directs behavior through its control of the motor apparatus.

ELECTROCONVULSIVE THERAPY (E.C.T., ELECTROSHOCK THERAPY)

A method of treatment of psychiatric disorders by passing an electric current through the brain, producing an artificial seizure.

ELECTROENCEPHALOGRAPH

An instrument, based on the string galvanometer, for measuring very small changes in potential derived from the electrical activity of the neurons of the brain. *Electroencephalogram,* the record obtained with the electroencephalograph, a "brain-wave tracing."

EMPATHY

(1) An objective awareness of the feelings, emotions, and behavior of another person. To be distinguished from sympathy, which is usually nonobjective and noncritical.

(2) A deep recognition of the significance of another person's behavior, which retains a certain objectivity and yet involves intellectual, emotional and motivational experiences corresponding to those of the other person.

ENVIRONMENT

All that surrounds the individual, including living and non-living, material and immaterial elements.

EPILEPSY

A disorder characterized by periodic seizures, and sometimes accompanied by a loss of consciousness. May be caused by organic or emotional disturbances.

Major epilepsy (grand mal) - Characterized by gross convulsive seizures, with loss of consciousness.

Minor epilepsy (petit mal) - Minor nonconvulsive epileptic seizures; may be limited to only momentary lapses of consciousness.

ETHOLOGY

The scientific study of the instincts. *Ethologist,* one who makes a scientific study of the instincts.

ETIOLOGY

Pertaining to causation; in medicine and nursing, pertaining to the causation of disease.

EUPHORIA

(1) An exaggerated feeling of physical and emotional well-being inconsonant with reality.

(2) An exaggerated (unrealistic) sense of well-being.

EXHIBITIONISM

Erotic pleasure in exposing the body to the view of others; in adults, a form of perversion when it is the principal form of erotic expression.

EXTROVERSION

A state in which attention and energies are largely directed outward from the self, as opposed to interest primarily directed toward the self, as in introversion.

F

FACULTY

A power or a function, especially a mental one.

FAMILY TRIANGLE

The situation, involving the child and the parents, in which the child experiences the wish to displace the parent of the same sex and possess the parent of the opposite sex. Family-triangle period, a developmental phase characterized by maximum intensity of these strivings. Synonymous with *Oedipal period*.

FANTASY (PHANTASY)

An image -- conscious or unconscious -- formed by recombinations of memories and interpretations of them.

FEAR

An experience, having both psychological and physiologic components, stimulated by the awareness of impending danger in the environment.

FIXATION

The persistence into later life of interests and behavior patterns appropriate to an earlier developmental phase.

FLATNESS OF AFFECT

A lack of normal emotional responsiveness, especially characteristic of *schizophrenia*.

FLIGHT OF IDEAS

A morbid type of thought sequence manifested through speech, characterized by its rapidity and by numerous and sudden shifts in topics, but that tends to be comprehensible to the normal observer. Typical of mania.

FREE ASSOCIATION

(1) In psychoanalytic therapy, spontaneous, uncensored verbalization by the patient of whatever comes to mind.

(2) A technic, used in *psychoanalysis,* in which the patient reports verbally his thoughts, emotions and sensations in whatever order they occur, making no effort at deliberate organization, censorship, or control.

FRUSTRATION

A blocking or nongratification of needs.

FUGUE

A major state of personality dissociation characterized by amnesia and actual physical flight from the immediate environment.

FUNCTIONAL

Pertaining solely or primarily to function. *Functional psychosis,* a psychosis occurring on the basis of disturbed mental functioning in the absence of structural brain damage.

G

GARRULOUSNESS

Excessive talkativeness, especially about trivial things.

GENITAL PHASE (OF DEVELOPMENT)

In psychoanalytic terminology, a synonym for emotional maturity.

GROUP

Any two or more persons who are set off from others, either temporarily or permanently, by a special type of association (relationship), as, for example, an important common interest.

Group therapy, a form of *psychotherapy* taking place among a group of patients under the guidance of a therapist.

H

HALLUCINATION

A sensory experience, occurring (in the absence of adequate reality-testing) on the basis of the subject's inner needs and independently of stimulation from the environment.

HALLUCINOGEN

A chemical substance capable of inducing hallucinations.

HEBEPHRENIA

One of the classic schizophrenic subgroups, the one having the most ominous prognosis. *Hebephrenic schizophrenia* is a synonym.

HEREDITARY

Genetically transmitted from parent to offspring.

HETEROSEXUAL

Pertaining to the opposite sex.

HOMEOSTASIS

A tendency to uniformity and stability in the normal body states of the organism (Walter B. Cannon).

HOMOSEXUAL

(adj.) Pertaining to an erotic interest in members of one's own sex. (noun) One having an erotic interest in members of his own sex.

(1) Sexual attraction or relationship between members of the same sex.

Latent homosexuality - A condition characterized by unconscious homosexual desires.

Overt homosexuality - Homosexuality that is consciously recognized or practiced.

(2) *Homosexuality,* a condition characterized by the subject's having an erotic interest in members of his own sex, a form of *personality disorder.*

HYPNOSIS (HYPNOTIC TRANCE)

(1) A state of increased receptivity to suggestion and direction, initially induced by the

influence of another person. The degree may vary from mild suggestibility to a trance state so profound as to be used in surgical operations.

(2) An artificially induced state, akin to sleep, in which the subject enters into so close a relationship with the hypnotist that the suggestions of the latter become virtually indistinguishable from the activity of his own ego.

HYPOCHONDRIASIS

(1) Overconcern with the state of physical or emotional health, accompanied by various bodily complaints without demonstrable organic pathology.

(2) A severe type of *psychoneurosis*, characterized by a morbid preoccupation with one's body and a partial withdrawal of interest from the environment. *Hypochondriac*, one afflicted with hypochondriasis.

HYSTERIA

A *psychoneurosis;* the older term for the conditions now designated as *conversion reaction* and *dissociative reaction*.

HYSTERICAL PERSONALITY

(1) A personality type characterized by shifting emotional feelings, susceptibility to suggestion, impulsive behavior, attention seeking, immaturity, and self-absorption; not necessarily disabling.

(2) A form of *personality disorder (neurotic personality)* characterized by conflicts and defenses similar to those found in persons with hysteria.
Hysteric, one afflicted with hysteria.

I

ID

The one of the three agencies or aspects of the mind that contains the psychic representations of the instinctual drives.

IDEATION

The process of forming ideas.

IDENTIFICATION

The adoption -- unconsciously -- of some of the characteristics of another person. Strictly speaking, the term refers to the result of the defense mechanism of *introjection*. (Sometimes identification and introjection are used loosely as synonyms.)

ILLUSION

A false perceptual experience occurring in response to an environmental stimulus; usually a symptom of serious mental illness.

INCEST

Culturally prohibited sexual relations between members of a family, usually persons closely related by blood, as father and daughter, mother and son, or brother and sister. INHIBITION

(1) Interference with or restriction of activities; the result of an unconscious defense against forbidden instinctual drives.

(2) The restraining or the stopping of a process; in psychiatry, the term usually refers to an inner force that opposes the gratification of a basic drive.

INSANITY

Now a term of legal or medicolegal significance only, referring to a mental disorder of sufficient gravity to bring the subject under special legal restrictions and immunities.

INSIGHT

(1) Self-understanding. A major goal of psychotherapy. The extent of the individual's understanding of the origin, nature, and mechanisms of his attitudes and behavior.

(2) In the broad psychiatric sense, the patient's knowledge that he suffers from an emo-

tional illness; in the narrow psychiatric sense, the patient's knowledge of the specific, hitherto unconscious, meaning of his symptom(s) or of some other aspect of illness.

INSTINCT

A term of many meanings; in dynamic psychiatric usage it is usually considered as synonymous with *basic drive.*

INSULIN COMA THERAPY

A method of treatment of psychoses through the induction of a series of comas by means of insulin injections.

INTERNALIZE

To place within (the mind). Said of a conflict or a state of tension that, in its original form, existed between an individual and some aspect of his environment, but that has come to exist within the mind (i.e., between one aspect of the personality and another). Thus *anxiety* is often found to be an *internalized fear.*

INTERPERSONAL

Existing between two or more individuals; often contrasted with intrapersonal.

INTERPRETATION

A scientific guess, made by a psychotherapist about a patient, explaining some aspect of the latter's thoughts, feelings or behavior.

INTRAPERSONAL (INTRAPSYCHIC)

Existing within a mind or a personality; often contrasted with *interpersonal.*

INTROJECTION

One of the *defense mechanisms;* the psychological process whereby a quality or an attribute of another person is taken into and made a part of the subject's personality (unconsciously). Often used loosely as synonymous with *identification.*

INVOLUTION (INVOLUTIONAL PERIOD)

A period in late middle age in which retrogressive physiologic changes take place, causing a loss of the capacity for reproduction. *Involutional psychosis,* a psychosis for which a major precipitating factor has been the advent of involution.

ISOLATION

One of the *defense mechanisms;* the psychological process whereby the actual facts of an experience are allowed to remain in consciousness, but the linkage between these facts and the related emotions or impulses is broken.

L

LATENCY (LATENCY PERIOD)

One of the phases of human development, occurring between the *family-triangle period* and *puberty* (approximately, ages 6 to 11 or 12 years), characterized by a relative instinctual quiescence coupled with a rapid intellectual development.

LEVELS OF AWARENESS (LEVELS OF CONSCIOUSNESS)

An expression referring to the fact that mental activity takes place with varying degrees of the subject's awareness: an individual may be entirely unaware, dimly aware, or fully aware of a given bit of mental activity.

LIBIDO

An inclusive term for the sexual-social drives.

LOBOTOMY (PREFRONTAL)

A psychosurgical procedure in which certain tracts of the brain are severed, thus stopping the interaction between the prefrontal areas (of the cerebral cortex) and the rest of the brain. Sometimes used as a therapeutic measure in severe psychoses.

LOOSENESS OF ASSOCIATION

A symptom of serious mental illness, usually of *schizophrenia,* in which the logical connections between a patient's successive thoughts are absent or are not discernible to the observer.

M

MALADJUSTMENT
A state of disequilibrium between the individual and his environment, in which his needs are not being gratified.

MALINGER
To feign an illness.

Malingerer, one who feigns an illness.

MANIA
(1) A suffix denoting a pathological preoccupation with some desire, idea, or activity; a morbid compulsion. Some frequently encountered manias are: *dipsomania,* compulsion to drink alcoholic beverages; *egomania,* pathological preoccupation with self; *kleptomania,* compulsion to steal; *megalomania,* pathological preoccupation with delusions of power or wealth; *monomania,* pathological preoccupation with one subject; *necromania,* pathological preoccupation with the dead; pyromania, morbid compulsion to set fires.

(2) A morbid state of extreme euphoria and excitement with loss of reality-testing; one of the phases of *manic-depressive psychosis.*

Manic (adj.), pertaining to mania; (noun), one who suffers from mania.

MANIC-DEPRESSIVE REACTION
A group of psychiatric disorders marked by conspicuous mood swings, ranging from normal to elation or to depression, or alternating. Officially regarded as a psychosis but may also exist in milder form.

Depressed phase - Characterized by depression of mood with retardation and inhibition of thinking and physical activity.

Manic phase - Characterized by depression of mood with retardation of thought, speech, and bodily motion, and by elation or grandiosity of mood, and irritability.

MASOCHISM
(1) Pleasure derived from undergoing physical or psychological pain inflicted by oneself or by others. It may be consciously sought or unconsciously arranged or invited. Present to some degree in all human relations and to greater degrees in all psychiatric disorders. It is the converse of sadism, in which pain is inflicted on another, and the two tend to coexist in the same individual.

(2) Finding gratification in pain; in the narrow sense, one of the perversions.

MASTURBATION
Erotic stimulation of one's external genitalia.

MATURITY
The state of being fully adult; psychologically characterized particularly by the ability to love others in a relatively non-selfish way.

MECHANISM (MENTAL, DEFENSE)
See Defense Mechanism.

MILIEU
The total environment, emotional as well as physical.

Milieu therapy, treatment by means of controlled modifications of the patient's environment.

MIND
The body in action as a unit. *Mental,* pertaining to mind as thus defined. *Mental illness,* accurately speaking, any illness of the mind, regardless of severity; often incorrectly restricted to severe psychiatric conditions.

MOTIVATION

A psychological state that incites to action.

MOURNING

The process that follows upon the loss of a love object, through which the subject gradually frees himself from the disequilibrium caused by the loss.

MULTIPLE PERSONALITY

A morbid condition, related to *dissociative reaction,* in which the normal organization of the personality is split up into distinct portions, all having a fairly complex organization of their own. (If there are only two such portions, the term dual personality is used.)

MUSCLE-TRAINING PERIOD

One of the developmental stages, lasting from the end of *infancy* to the beginning of the *family-triangle period* (about age 1½ to age 3), during which the child receives training in sphincter control and other motor activities. Synonymous with *anal period*.

MYELIN

The fatlike substance that forms a sheath around the medullated nerve fibers. *Myelinization,* the process of acquiring a myelin sheath.

N

NARCISSISM (NARCISM)

(1) Self-love, as opposed to object-love (love of another person). Some degree of narcissism is considered healthy and normal, but an excess interferes with relations with others.

(2) Self-love; extreme narcissism is the emotional position found in the newborn infant and in certain psychoses. The term is derived from the Greek legend of Narcissus, a youth who fell in love with his own image.

Narcissistic, loving oneself excessively in a childish or an infantile fashion.

NARCOSYNTHESIS

A form of psychiatric treatment in which contact is established with the patient while he is under the influence of a hypnotic drug.

NEGATIVISM

A tendency to resist suggestions or requests, often accompanied by a response that is, in some sense, the opposite of the one sought. *Negativistic,* expressing negativism.

NEOLOGISM

A newly coined word, or the act of coining such a word; a phenomenon seen in *schizophrenia* and in some cases of *organic brain disease*.

NEURASTHENIA

One of the psychoneuroses, related to *anxiety reaction,* characterized by chronic feelings of fatigue and tension and often by disturbances in the sexual function and minor disturbances in the digestive function.

NEUROPHYSIOLOGY

The physiology of the nervous sytem. *Neurophysiologist,* a specialist in neurophysiology.

NEUROSIS

See psychoneurosis.

O

OBJECT

A term with several meanings. In the broadest sense, it is used in contrast with the term *subject* and means anything in the environment, including another person. In a narrower sense, *object* refers to "a satisfying something" in the environment that is capable of offering instinctual gratification. Thus, *love object* refers to a person toward whom the subject experiences libidinal strivings.

OBSESSION
(1) Persistent, unwanted idea or impulse that cannot be eliminated by logic or reasoning.
(2) A thought, recognized by the subject as more or less irrational, that persistently recurs, despite the subject's conscious wish to avoid or ignore it.
obsessive, pertaining to or afflicted with obsessions.

OBSESSIVE-COMPULSIVE NEUROSIS
One of the psychoneuroses, characterized by *obsessions* and *compulsions* and an underlying personality type whose conflicts involve problems of the muscle-training period.

OEDIPUS
A character in Greek legend, who unwittingly killed his father and married his mother and was subsequently punished by the gods by being blinded. *Oedipus complex,* a term referring to the erotic attachment of the (normal as well as neurotic) small child to the parent of the opposite sex, repressed largely because of the fear of bodily mutilation ("castration") by the presumedly jealous parent of the same sex. *Oedipal period,* same as *family-triangle period.*

ORAL PERIOD
The first postuterine developmental period, roughly synonymous with infancy, in which the individual's central experiences are those involved in the act of sucking.

ORAL PERSONALITY
One of the *personality disorders,* characterized by the persistence in adult life of problems and defenses appropriate to the *oral period* of development.

ORGANIC
Based on structural alterations, gross or microscopic. *Organic psychosis,* a psychosis the etiology of which involves structural damage. (The term also includes *toxic psychosis,* in which the physical alterations are at a submicroscopic -- i.e., chemical -- level.)

ORGANISM
A general term for any living creature, including man.

OVERCOMPENSATION
A conscious or unconscious process in which a real or fancied physical or psychological deficit inspires exaggerated correction.

OVERT
Discernible; "out in the open."

P

PANIC (PANIC REACTION)
A morbid state characterized by extreme fear and/or anxiety, causing a temporary disorganization of the personality.

PARANOIA
Traditionally considered to be one of the three major functional (nonorganic) psychoses, but now generally thought to be one variety of paranoid schizophrenia. A pathologic state, characterized by extreme suspiciousness and highly organized delusions of persecution, occurring in the presence of a clear sensorium and relatively appropriate affective responses.

Paranoid, pertaining to paranoia or paranoid schizophrenia.

Paranoid reaction, an acute, often self-limited state, resembling paranoia; the term is inclusive of paranoid syndromes arising on the basis of organic disease.

PARANOID SCHIZOPHRENIA
One of the four major schizophrenic subgroups, characterized by the usual features of *schizophrenia* plus delusions of persecution and/or grandeur (often loosely organized), auditory hallucinations in keeping with the delusions, and a marked, generalized suspiciousness.

PARANOID STATE
Characterized by delusions of persecution. A paranoid state may be of short duration or

chronic.

PATHOGENESIS

The mode of development of disease states.

PERCEPTION

A psychological experience in which sensory stimuli are integrated to form an image (the significance of which is influenced by past experiences).

PERSONALITY

The whole group of adjustment technics and equipment that are characteristic for a given individual in meeting the various situations of life.

PERSONALITY DISORDER

In the limited (diagnostic) sense, a type of psychiatric illness in which the patient's inner difficulties are revealed, not by specific symptoms but by an unhealthy pattern of living. Thus used, roughly synonymous with *character disorder* and *behavior disorder.* In a broader sense, "disorder of the personality" is often used as equivalent to "mental illness" or "emotional illness:'

PERVERSION (SEXUAL PERVERSION)

A form of personality disorder, characterized by an alteration from the normal of the *aim* and/or the *object* of libidinal strivings. Examples: *sadism, masochism, voyeurism.*

PHANTASY

See fantasy.

PHOBIA

(1) An obsessive, unrealistic fear of an external object or situation. Some of the common phobias are *acrophobia,* fear of heights; *agoraphobia,* fear of open places; claustrophobia, fear of closed spaces; *mysophobia,* fear of dirt and germs; *xenophobia, fear* of *strangers.*

(2) The dread of an object, an act or a situation that is not realistically dangerous, but that has come to represent a danger.
Phobic, pertaining to phobias.

PHOBIC REACTION

One of the psychoneuroses, formerly called *anxiety hysteria,* characterized by the presence of phobias.

PRECONSCIOUS

One of the three levels of *awareness,* the quality attaching to an idea, a sensation or an emotion of which the subject is not spontaneously aware but can become aware with effort.

PREMORBID PERSONALITY

The status of an individual's personality (conflicts, defenses, strengths, weaknesses) before the onset of clinical illness.

PRIMARY GAIN

The adjustment (adaptational) value of a neurotic symptom per se.

PROJECTION

One of the *defense mechanisms,* a technic whereby feelings, wishes or attitudes, originating within the subject, are attributed by him to persons or other objects in his environment.

PROJECTIVE TESTS

(1) Psychological tests used as a diagnostic tool. Among the most common projective tests is the Rorschach (inkblot) test.

(2) A relatively unstructured, although standardized, psychological test in which the subject is called upon to respond with a minimum of intellectual restrictions, thereby revealing characteristic drives, defenses and attitudes. (Examples are the Rorschach and the Thematic Apperception Tests.)

PSYCHE
Actually synonymous with *mind;* frequently used in expressions suggesting a mind-body duality, as, for example, "psychosomatic," "psychophysiologic," and "psychic versus organic factors:'

PSYCHIATRY
That branch of medicine that deals with the causes, the diagnosis, the treatment and the prevention of mental disorders.

Psychiatrist, a physician specializing in psychiatry.

Psychiatric nurse, a nurse specializing in the care of patients having mental disorders.

Psychiatric team, a group of professional and semiprofessional persons working together under the direction of a psychiatrist in the treatment of psychiatric, patients. (Usually the membership of such a team includes psychiatrist, psychiatric nurse, clinical psychologist, psychiatric social worker, occupational therapist, and psychiatric aide.)

PSYCHOANALYSIS
(1) A theory of human development and behavior, a method of research, and a system of psychotherapy, originally described by Sigmund Freud (1856-1939). Through analysis of free associations and interpretation of dreams, emotions and behavior are traced to the influence of repressed instinctual drives in the unconscious. Psychoanalytic treatment seeks to eliminate or diminish the undesirable effects of unconscious conflicts by making the patient aware of their existence, origin, and inappropriate expression.

(2) The term designates 1. a *method* of (a) psychotherapy and (b) psychological research, and 2. a body of *facts and theories* of human psychology. Both the method and the body of knowledge represent the work of Sigmund Freud and his followers. *Psychoanalyst,* a professional person, usually a physician, who has received specialized formal training in the theory and the practice of psychoanalysis.

PSYCHONEUROSIS (NEUROSIS)
(1) One of the two major categories of emotional illness, the other being the psychoses. It is usually less severe than a psychosis, with minimal loss of contact with reality.

(2) A mild to moderately severe illness of the personality (mind), in which the ego function of reality-testing is not gravely impaired, and in which the maladjustment to life is of a relatively limited nature.

Psychoneurotic, pertaining to or characteristic of a psychoneurosis.

PSYCHOPATHIC PERSONALITY
An older term for one of the varieties of *personality disorder,* roughly synonymous with the current (official) category of "sociopathic personality disturbance," a form of illness characterized by emotional immaturity, the use of short-term values and behavior that is asocial or antisocial.

PSYCHOSIS
(1) A major mental disorder of organic and/or emotional origin in which there is a departure from normal patterns of thinking, feeling, and acting. Commonly characterized by loss of contact with reality, distortion of perception, regressive behavior and attitudes, diminished control of elementary impulses and desires, and delusions and hallucinations. Chronic and generalized personality deterioration may occur. A majority of patients in public mental hospitals are psychotic.

(2) A very serious illness of the personality (mind), involving a major impairment of ego function, particularly with respect to reality-testing, and revealed by signs of a grave maladjustment to life.

Psychotic, pertaining to or afflicted with psychosis.

PSYCHOSOMATIC
Adjective to denote the constant and inseparable interdependence of the psyche (mind) and

the soma (body). Most commonly used to refer to illnesses in which the manifestations are primarily physical with at least a partial emotional cause.

PSYCHOSURGERY
A form of neurosurgery in which specific tracts or other limited portions of the brain are severed or destroyed with the intention of producing favorable effects upon the patient's psychological status.

PSYCHOTHERAPY
(1) The term for any type of mental treatment that is based primarily upon verbal or non-verbal communication with the patient in distinction to the use of drugs, surgery, or physical measures such as electric or insulin shock.

(2) A term with many shades of meaning. In the broadest sense it is equivalent to "psychological treatment measures;" in a narrower sense *psychotherapy* refers to a direct relationship between one or more patients and a professional person, the therapist, in which the latter endeavors "to provide new life experiences which can influence the patient in the direction of health" (Levine).

PSYCHOTIC PERSONALITY
A variety of personality disorder, synonymous with the current official term "personality pattern disturbance," in which, despite the absence of the usual clinical symptoms of psychosis, the individual's fundamental conflicts and defenses are those of a *psychotic*.

R

RATIONALIZATION
The process of constructing plausible reasons for one's responses (usually to avoid awareness of neurotic motives).

REACTION FORMATION
One of the *defense mechanisms,* a technic whereby an original attitude or set of feelings is replaced in consciousness by the opposite attitude or feelings.

REALITY-TESTING
The process of determining objective (usually external) reality, a function of the ego.

RECONSTITUTE
To form again. The term is used of a personality that, having become more or less disorganized through illness, resumes its previous defense measures and type of adjustment.

REGRESSION
(1) The partial or symbolic return to more infantile patterns of reacting.

(2) One of the *defense mechanisms;* a process in which the personality retraces developmental steps, moving backward to earlier interests, defenses, and modes of gratification.

REPRESSION
(1) A defense mechanisms, operating unconsciously, that banishes unacceptable ideas, emotions, or impulses from consciousness or that keeps out of consciousness what has never been conscious.

(2) One of the *defense mechanisms,* a technic whereby thoughts, emotions and/or sensations are thrust out of consciousness.

REVERSAL
One of the *defense mechanisms,* a technic whereby an instinctual impulse is seemingly turned into its opposite, as, for example, when *sadism* is replaced by *masochism*.

S

SADISM

A form of perversion characterized by the experiencing of erotic pleasure in inflicting pain on another person. Often used more broadly as meaning the enjoyment of cruelty. *(See* Masochism.)

SCHIZOID

Schizophrenic-like. *Schizoid personality,* a form of *personality disorder* (subgroup of *psychotic personality)* characterized by withdrawn, self-centered, often eccentric behavior.

SCHIZOPHRENIA

(1) A severe emotional disorder of psychotic depth, characteristically marked by a retreat from reality with delusion formation, hallucinations, emotional disharmony, and regressive behavior. Formerly called dementia praecox. Its prognosis has improved in recent years.

(2) One of the major *functional psychoses;* more accurately, a group of interrelated symptom syndromes, having in common a number of features, including *associative looseness, autistic thinking, ambivalence* and inappropriateness of *affect*. The classic subgroups are: *catatonic, paranoid, simple* and *hebephrenic* schizophrenia; other varieties are: *schizoaffective, undifferentiated, childhood* and *latent* schizophrenia. *Schizophrenic,* pertaining to or afflicted with schizophrenia.

SECONDARY GAIN

The adjustment value or gratification that occurs as a result of the way in which a patient's environment responds to his illness (not an integral part of the symptoms per se).

SELF-CONCEPT

A person's image of himself, usually his conscious image.

SENILE

Pertaining to (extreme) old age, particularly to the deterioration in adjustment capacity occurring in old age.

Senile psychosis, an organic psychosis resulting from the brain damage accompanying advanced age.

SHOCK TREATMENT

A form of psychiatric treatment in which electric current, insulin, or carbon dioxide is administered to the patient and results in a convulsive reaction to alter favorably the course of mental illness.

SIMPLE SCHIZOPHRENIA

One of the four classic *schizophrenia* subgroups, characterized by slow, insidious onset and chronic course, with the illness being shown by emotional coldness, withdrawal and eccentricity, rather than by more striking symptoms.

SOMATOPSYCHIC

A term of recent coinage, intended to indicate psychological effects of somatic pathology.

SPLIT PERSONALITY

A term calling attention to the schizophrenic's inappropriate-ness of affect; the "split" is thus between emotions and ideation.

STRESS

Any circumstance that taxes the adjustment capacity of the individual.

SUBJECT
The person under discussion or study, as, for example, a patient or a person upon whom an experiment is performed.

SUBLIMATION
(1) A defense mechanism, operating unconsciously, by which instinctual but consciously unacceptable drives are diverted into personally and socially acceptable channels.
(2) One of the *defense mechanisms,* the only one that is never pathogenic; a technic whereby the original aim or *object* of a basic drive is altered in a manner that allows the release of tension and, at the same time, is socially acceptable.

SUPEREGO
One of the three major aspects or agencies of the mind; similar to the term "conscience" but more inclusive since it involves both conscious and unconscious components. (*See* Ego.)

SUPPRESSION
A technic of adjustment -- differing from the *defense mechanisms* in that it is fully conscious and very rarely pathogenic -- whereby the ego denies expression to a thought or an impulse. (It is often contrasted with *repression,* which is automatic, unconsciously effected and frequently pathogenic.)

SYMBOLISM
The use of one mental image to represent another.

T

TOXIC
Pertaining to, or due to the action of, a poison.

Toxic *psychosis,* a psychosis brought about by the action of a poisonous substance or, more broadly, a psychosis brought about by any chemical interference with normal metabolic processes (grouped with the *organic psychoses*).

TRANSFERENCE
The attributing by the subject, to a figure in his current environment, of characteristics first encountered in some figure of his early life, and the experiencing of desires, fears, and other attitudes toward the current figure that originated in the relationship with the past figure. The term is most commonly used with respect to feelings of a patient toward his therapist.

Counter-transference, transference feelings of a therapist toward his patient.

TRAUMA
Harm or injury; sometimes, the circumstances productive of harm or injury. In psychiatry, the term is inclusive of purely emotional as well as physical injury.

Traumatic, harmful, pertaining to trauma.

TRAUMATIC NEUROSIS (WAR NEUROSIS)
An acute morbid reaction related to *psychoneurosis* but occurring only in response to overwhelming trauma or stress. The condition is characterized by a temporary, partial disorganization of the personality, followed by such symptoms as anxiety, restlessness, irritability, impaired concentration, evidence of autonomic dysfunction and repetitive nightmares in which the traumatic experience is "relived."

TURNING AGAINST THE SELF
One of the *defense mechanisms,* a technic in which an unacceptable drive (usually aggressive) is diverted from its original object and (unconsciously) made to operate against the self, in whole or in part.

U

UNCONSCIOUS
(1) That part of the mind the content of which is only rarely subject to awareness. It is the repository for knowledge that has never been conscious or that may have been conscious briefly and was then repressed.
(2) In psychiatry, one of the three *levels* of *awareness;* thoughts, sensations, and emotions at this level cannot enter the subject's awareness through any voluntary effort on his part, but they continue to exert effects upon his behavior.

UNDOING
One of the *defense mechanisms,* a technic in which a specific action is performed that is (unconsciously) considered by the subject to be in some sense the opposite of a previous unacceptable action (or wish), and thus to neutralize ("undo") the original action.

V

VEGETATIVE SIGNS (OF DEPRESSION)
A traditionally grouped set of findings, including anorexia, weight loss, constipation, amenorrhea, insomnia and "morning-evening variation in mood," that, when found in combination, are indicative of severe depression.

VOYEURISM
A form of *personality disorder* (more specifically, of *perversion),* in which the subject receives his principal erotic gratification in clandestine peeping.

W

WAXY FLEXIBILITY
A phenomenon, associated with *catatonic schizophrenia,* in which the body, particularly the extremities, will remain for long periods of time in any positions selected by the examiner.

www.ingramcontent.com/pod-product-compliance
Lightning Source LLC
Chambersburg PA
CBHW081816300426
44116CB00014B/2386